ENDORSEME [barcode] T0047499

This book is simply a supernatural masterpiece. One of the most important books of our time! It's written by a woman whose whole life belongs to Jesus and is saturated in His love and Presence. I encourage you, as you embark on this amazing journey, to read slowly, drinking in every word, allowing each piece of revelation and every activation to become a doorway for you to step through. Your life is about to completely transform.

LIZ WRIGHT
International speaker, mentor, podcast show
host, and best-selling author of *Reflecting God*
lizwright.org

One of the first things that the Gospels record Jesus saying to His followers is, *"I tell you, you will see Heaven open, and the angels of God ascending and descending on the Son of Man"* (John 1:51). Yet so few of us believe that we can seek this revelation and we haven't been taught how to grow in it. Sarah-Jane leads us into the realm of the Spirit with inspiring stories, biblical insight, and practical steps to take. Read it and prepare to have the veil of unbelief and confusion removed and your relationship with the Lord of Heaven deepen and expand.

REV. CANON JOHN McGINLEY
New Wine, Head of Church Planting Development

Anytime you have the privilege to pray with or listen to Sarah-Jane speak, you will encounter passion, authority, revelation, and practical no-nonsense action! Her first book *Seeing*

Beyond is ten chapters of instruction laced with practical activity points and prayer all the way through. SJ shares her heart that loves the call of the pioneer and explorer and says "yes" to adventuring with God into the previously unknown and unseen places. In this book, *Seeing Beyond,* she stirs the reader to join her on this journey of having your senses trained and becoming aware of the unseen, invisible realm. This book will challenge the way you pray and how you see your world!

RACHEL HICKSON
Founder and director, Heartcry for Change

Sarah-Jane is the real deal; she hears from God and does so in a truly down-to-earth way. God has used her faithful prayers and powerful revelatory gift to catalyse and confirm at significant moments in my life. This book is the real deal too. If you are game for exploring the deeper things of God and up for an adventure, you will find this book inspirational, applicable, and potentially life-changing. Enjoy.

KARL MARTIN
International speaker, coach
Author of *Lead* and *Stand*

It has been a genuine honor and privilege to run relationally with Sarah Jane in equipping the saints to do the work of the ministry. She is a woman of noble character and operates in the gifts of the Spirit with love, grace, and power. Her writing carries the weight of one who not only knows the Word, but lives it out.

Sarah Jane's book *Seeing Beyond* takes you on an incredible journey of discovery and training of your senses to be fixed on the unseen realm. Powerful and impactful!

With profound insight this book guides the reader in the "how-tos" of seeing beyond and experiencing more in the realm of the spirit. The practical application and personalized prayers in this book are truly transformational. We believe that an incredibly gifted and courageous generation is being awakened, and this book will serve powerfully in equipping them to navigate in the realm from which they have been created to rule and reign.

For such a time as this!

STEVEN AND RENE SPRINGER
Global Presence Ministries

"While we look not at the things which are seen, but at the things which are not seen; for the things which are seen are temporal, but the things which are not seen are eternal" (2 Corinthians 4:18 NASB). The spirit realm is alive and active. It is real and buzzing with activity 24 hours a day, 7 days a week. It is never on vacation. God is always about His business of His Kingdom. And His business is ruling the entire universe for an eternity. The throne of our Heavenly Father and His realm of eternity, literally and continually vibrates with divine activity. For us to be effective sons and daughters in His Kingdom we must not ignore the most active part of His creation. Why? If God is concerned about the spirit realm and He resides in the eternal spirit realm, and our position is one of heirs of God and co-heirs with Christ, then it is our inherited promise to know, behold and see beyond into the spiritual realities of His Kingdom. Thank you Sarah-Jane for this insightful and empowering teaching. It is a timely message and is so beautifully written. Each of you reading *Seeing Beyond* will be empowered through scriptural truths and activated to behold,

see, grow, and mature in your ability to "see the unseen," to experience beautiful encounters with Him, and to bring transformation to the world in which we live.

REBECCA GREENWOOD
Cofounder, Christian Harvest International
Strategic Prayer Apostolic Network
International Freedom Group

Seeing Beyond is one of the most practical and revelatory books on the prophetic that I have ever read! It makes the often over-mystified "seer realm" available and accessible to all spiritually hungry believers. Every Christian is able to see in the spirit because we have the Holy Spirit living within us. Sarah-Jane issues a wonderful invitation to everyone ready to biblically and experientially engage this realm of the prophetic. And I do believe *Seeing Beyond* will prove to be a valuable contribution to the unfolding conversation about defining and demonstrating the seer anointing.

Larry Sparks, MDiv
Publisher, Destiny Image

I have ministered alongside Sarah-Jane and have seen firsthand her accuracy in the prophetic and her wisdom in communicating complicated truths. Sarah-Jane's unique gifting is not just a special gift that was given to her, instead she submitted herself to the training of the Lord to develop it into something the Lord can use to accomplish His will and purposes. Now she is taking what the Lord showed her and using it to train you.

I highly recommend this book to equip you to develop and grow your prophetic seer gift.

Jennifer LeClaire
Author, *Cleansing Your Home from Evil*

From the beginning of time, God has longed for a pure relationship with mankind. Here in this book, Sarah-Jane not only inspires you to know God more intimately (John 17:3), but also gives you practical steps, chapter after chapter, on how you can commune with God and hear His voice more clearly. Jesus reveals Himself to those who prepare themselves (Revelation 19:8-10) and this book will help you "get ready" to encounter a living God. I commend it to you and commend you to go deeper and further with Him.

STACEY CAMPBELL
Shiloh Global
www.wesleystaceycampbell.com

"What is out there?" is something that so many people want to understand today—Christian and non-Christian alike. In *Seeing Beyond* Sarah-Jane Biggart shows herself to be a trusted and experienced guide who is able to help people develop their seer prophetic gifting. Chapter by chapter Sarah-Jane helps to open our spiritual eyes and see what is really happening. It is a vital gift not just to see but to truly perceive, indeed to understand. Through clear biblical teaching, personal example, and activation prayers, Sarah-Jane helps us to step out boldly on this adventure with God.

ALAN MCWILLIAM
CEO & Team Lead for Cairn
Movement and Forge European Director

"If you see the invisible you will do the impossible," encapsulates the essence of this groundbreaking book. Sarah-Jane writes graciously, with a mix of sensitivity, passion and inspiration. At the same time it is provocative, for there is a necessity not only to perceive, but an exhortation to allow "seeing beyond" to become part of us. This is not just a manual with excellent practical teaching and activation exercises, but it is a statement of intent to motivate us to seek God for more, as the unseen realm is opened. It is an incisive challenge which will sharpen awareness of the reality that actually matters, and to engender a hunger for greater revelation of the unseen. "Lord, open our eyes that we may see."

STEVE HEPDEN MTH

In *Seeing Beyond*, Sarah-Jane takes us on an adventure with Jesus that many of us have read in Scripture is possible and have perhaps dreamed of but have never had the guidance or encouragement on how to take our first steps into. If you are curious about the unseen realm—and I believe that we all should be—I know that you will find this book immensely helpful, practical, authentic, and real. That is because Sarah-Jane is each of these things! She's the real deal as a mum, wife, leader, minister, businesswoman, watchman prophet, and seer and is uncompromising and passionate in all these areas!

DAVID STARK
Co-Director, Global Prophetic
Alliance & Power Church, Glasgow

SEEING BEYOND

How to Make Supernatural Sight Your Daily Reality

SARAH-JANE BIGGART

DESTINY IMAGE® PUBLISHERS, INC.

P.O. Box 310, Shippensburg, PA 17257-0310

"Promoting Inspired Lives."

This book and all other Destiny Image and Destiny Image Fiction books are available at Christian bookstores and distributors worldwide.

Cover design by Eileen Rockwell

Interior design by Terry Clifton

For more information on foreign distributors, call 717-532-3040.

Reach us on the Internet: www.destinyimage.com.

ISBN 13 TP: 978-0-7684-5894-7

ISBN 13 eBook: 978-0-7684-5895-4

ISBN 13 HC: 978-0-7684-5897-8

ISBN 13 LP: 978-0-7684-5896-1

For Worldwide Distribution, Printed in the U.S.A.

3 4 5 6 7 8 / 25 24 23 22

DEDICATION

To all of those who have counted the cost
of the pursuit of Jesus Christ and said yes.

To all those finding their way to Jesus
Christ, the only way to fullness of life.
The way is open to all who seek Him.

To my family—

My beloved Alastair, Thomas and Sophie who have made room, supported and agreed with the work of God in my life, cheered me on and celebrated every word count and chapter of *Seeing Beyond* as it was written. I love you all dearly and thank God for you.

To Emma and David Stark for your consistent trust in me: for loving in and through all seasons, making room for all aspects of growth and championing me in all aspects of my pursuit for more of the Lord. Emma, I thank God for hearts bonded and lives lived together for the glory of God. I am forever grateful to the Lord for this precious gift.

For all who have gone before 'into the unknown' for showing us the way; those celebrated and remembered and those forgotten. We celebrate all pioneers and the pursuit of discovery—may we each be spurred on to keep exploring!

Acknowledgments

Larry Sparks—for your fierce determination to call people into their authorships—thank you. Without your invitation this book would still be inside me! Thank you for championing me and many others.

Fiona Rackstraw—what a joy and delight to work on this book with you after all these years. You are a gift! Thank you for your diligent, focused editing and insight.

Thank you, Destiny Image team, for bringing the book to life. You are amazing.

Open up, ancient gates!

Open up, ancient doors,

and let the King of glory enter.

PSALM 24:9 NLT

CONTENTS

FOREWORD

Lord, I pray, open his eyes that he might see.
—2 KINGS 6:17

ONE SUNDAY MORNING DURING PRAYER I SAW A BOXING RING with two demons dancing around inside the ropes. One was named The Destroyer and the other The Devourer. They were not fighting one another but rather were taunting the crowd of onlookers saying, "Why doesn't one of you come and fight me?" As I looked at the crowd, I recognised the faces of people from my church and other leaders in the Body of Christ; no one was taking up the challenge. I became frustrated, thinking, *I know these people. They are warriors. Why won't anyone get in the ring and knock their heads off and make them be quiet?* Yet no one moved. Then I saw why. The demons were wearing boxing robes which usually have the name of the fighter written on the back.

1

However, instead of their names, each demon's robe had these simple words written clearly on the back: "This Is Just Life."

It then occurred to me that the otherwise bold spiritual warriors were not engaging in fighting these demons because they believed the lie—that their challenges, sicknesses, and losses were not a spiritual attack but rather were "just life." For example, it's just life when you get older and your body starts to break down and get sick. It's just life when you send your children off to university and they get caught up with the wrong crowd. It's just life to struggle financially in a challenging economy.

Suddenly I heard the Voice of the Lord, say, "This is not just life! The Destroyer is wreaking havoc on the lives of My people. The Devourer is robbing them of their health, their wealth, and their families. Wake up and fight!"

God's promise to His church on the Day of Pentecost was that when the Holy Spirit was poured out, they could function under a revelation anointing of dreams, visions, and prophecy. It was part of His equipping tools that would enable believers to live victorious Christian lives in the midst of a dark and dangerous world. He knew we would need to be able to see into the spirit realm in order to position ourselves properly to advance the Kingdom of God on earth.

The early disciples learned to see beyond the persecution and see God's divine purpose. Paul saw beyond his temporal trials into the realm of eternal glory. John saw beyond the earthly realm into the heavenly realm. Stephen even saw beyond death into an open Heaven and into the very face of Jesus.

Today God is urging His people to wake up and see beyond their current circumstances, to accept His invitation to see into another realm. This mysterious unseen dimension is as real as the world around us; however, it must be accessed by spiritual eyes anointed by the Holy Spirit. Once spiritual sight is activated and acknowledged, a whole new world opens up, revealing the activity of angels, demons, and even God Himself. As in the vision above, once proper spiritual perspective is gained, it becomes easier strategically to advance God's Kingdom assignment, taking out every demonic opposing force.

In Second Kings 6 we are given a glimpse into this unseen realm. Elisha had been prophetically spying in the enemy's camp, seeing into their plans to fight the armies of Israel. Every time the Syrians would set an ambush Elisha would warn Israel not to fall into their trap. This infuriated the Syrian king and he ordered that the spy be found. One of his men informed him that it was not a spy but rather the prophet, Elisha, who kept revealing their plans; so, the king ordered his men to find Elisha and execute him.

That night, the Syrian armies surrounded the house where Elisha and his servant were staying. When the servant awakened, he looked out and saw the very real threat of the enemy. However, when he ran to Elisha to tell him of their fate, Elisha simply responded, "Don't worry, there are more that are with us than are with them." The servant thought, *More with us? There are hundreds of them and only two of us.* Then Elisha prayed, "Lord, open his eyes so he might see." And the Lord opened the eyes of Elisha's servant and he saw that there was a natural reality, that they were in fact surrounded. However, he also saw that there was a supernatural reality in that the mountains were actually filled with angel armies, horses and chariots of fire surrounding their enemy. The supernatural trumps the natural every time!

This book by Sarah-Jane Biggart could not be timelier! Her depth of biblical understanding and practical visionary experience will both equip and inspire you to press into a greater relationship with the Holy Spirit and see into the unseen dimension as never before. She will challenge you to discover your prophetic capabilities, knowing it is imperative for the people of God to open their eyes and begin to see beyond the natural realm into the supernatural. This will enlighten us so we can be on the offensive rather than playing defense against the enemy. It will enable us to unlock the hidden destinies of people, even cities and nations. It will empower us to co-labour with angel armies and to fulfill the will of God on earth as it is in the heavenly realm. *Seeing Beyond* will remove the veil from our eyes so that we can see Jesus, our Bridegroom, and fall in love with Him all over again. Lord, open our eyes so we may see! Let the journey begin!

JANE HAMON
Vision Church@Christian International, Florida
Author of *Dreams and Visions, Deborah Company, Discernment, Declarations for Breakthrough,* and *The Cyrus Decree*

FOREWORD

It was another normal, wet, and cold school day in late 1980s Northern Ireland. Nothing noteworthy was in my diary, but God was planning a pivot moment in my life as I joined the line to queue for lunch at the school canteen. My 14-year-old peers jostled for position, noisily debriefing with each other about the morning classes we had just come from. In this most ordinary of moments, I looked up and suddenly the entire natural world disappeared from my sight! All I could see before me were what I can only describe as "spirit-realm faces." Disembodied faces filled the walls, floor to ceiling. Some faces were beautiful and glorious, others were malevolent and malicious. As I now know, these were spirit watchers, pressed together; some were angelic, looking and guarding; some were demonic, observing and planning oppression.

I stumbled—food tray in hand—to the nearest table, mesmerized and slightly terrified. I was being watched—we were all being watched. Not just by God alone, high and lifted up, seated outside the circle of the earth on a throne. We were also being watched and shielded (and watched and hated in equal measure) in close proximity, live and in real time, by spiritual beings.

I was seen. And I was seeing things outside of the realm of the flesh. My physical frame started to shake as utter surprise and confusion reigned. I had so many questions in that moment: What was going on? Was this normal? Was it right? Was it helpful? Was I blessed, or was I cursed? My teenage brain raced—how did this happen?

The dazzling and unconventional reality of the spirit realm had just opened up to me.

It took me years to even talk about that moment, but it was the beginning of a life lived with eyes open to the spirit realm. God ordained that my eyes would open, just like Elisha's servant's eyes had in Second Kings 6. There then followed years of practice and biblical research for me to find language and skills of spirit realm navigation. Over this time I had yet more questions: What is allowed? What is not? How do we not get led astray? How do we react when we see the fire in the eyes of Jesus in real time?

I would love to somehow be able to reach back in time and give this book to my teenage self—this wonderful book that you are now holding! It would have saved me years of thinking that I was strange and I'm sure that it would have calmed those raging doubts I had, where I wondered if I really was in the centre of God's will when it came to being able to see into the spirit realm.

My younger self didn't have anyone to teach me or safely guide me in all of this, but happily now *you* do! Sarah-Jane will remarkably hold you by the hand as you read this book. She will answer your questions, give you instruction to keep you from harm, and will give you good, biblical boundaries to help steer you deeper into the realms of seeing by the Holy Spirit.

You and I are predominantly and essentially spirit beings. As believers in Jesus, our spirits will live forever. It is only our flesh that is a temporary part of us. We tend to think of ourselves as more flesh and bone than spirit, and yet, at our creation, we were made not just from the physical dust of the earth but also from the breath of God! God blew His breath into Adam and the breath of God in us made us living spirits, with a spirit dimension. God gave Adam (and then subsequently us) the substance of another dimension—the substance of His spirit realm! Adam's three-dimensional earthly existence was given a heavenly dimension of spirit in it. You are God-breathed spirit at your core.

God is re-sensitizing us to the details and reality of the realm that He inhabits. We must think of ourselves afresh—as spirit beings first and foremost. It's time to think of our earthly bodies as our secondary identity, not our primary identity. It's time for you to be released fully as a spirit being who interacts with the spiritual realm, as much as you are a fleshly being who interacts with the physical realm. This is not just to be your reality when you die. Spiritual sight is your inheritance now, while you're still on the earth.

The New Testament of the Bible does more than merely suggest that spiritual sight is good for you. It actually *commands* it to become your reality. It sets seeing in the spirit the standard for biblical normality. As Paul writes:

So we fix our eyes not on what is seen, but on what is unseen, since what is seen is temporary, but what is unseen is eternal (2 Corinthians 4:18).

The cry to fix your eyes on what is unseen is being shouted over your life! You are to gaze beyond bricks and walls, bones and skin, and see the structures, layers, and truth of the heavenly realms. The cry to fix your eyes on what is unseen is pulling you today, so that you might not miss out on seeing the Throne Room of God, the myriad of heavenly hosts, the Holy City, guardian angels, spirit horses, rooms in the Court of God, Divine Council chambers, the face of Jesus Christ Himself—and all the other infinite wonders that God has in His remarkable Kingdom.

Sarah-Jane's life journey has often left me filled with awe. I do hope you will meet her in person one day! She sees in the spirit realm like no one else I know. Her discernment is so sharp in how to deal with what she is seeing. Hers is a life of set apart devotion, unwavering love, and focus on Jesus. She is a gift to the body of Christ and to you, dear reader.

Sarah-Jane and I have travelled and ministered together for many years. We've done life together—as mums, as female pioneers, and as friends. I trust her with my life—and I literally mean this. Sarah-Jane will walk into a room and immediately see what the angels are doing, know what God is planning, and will have insight into what the demons are releasing to derail the people of God. Her sight has rescued many from destruction and orientated many more into the full plans of God for their lives. Sarah-Jane has undoubtedly kept me safe and sharpened many times over by this ability to go beyond the boundaries of the realms of the flesh. Her faithfulness, courage, generosity, submission, willingness to serve, and her unceasing prayers have supported me through both the highest of times and the most challenging of times.

As you begin this journey of "seeing beyond," please know that Sarah-Jane is a model for how *your* life can be! Seeing into the spirit realm is not reserved just for Old Testament characters. It is not antiquated or strange, it is vital and *biblically normal.* We tend to relegate spiritual sight to the so-called "greats" of old who are long dead and gone and we get ourselves stuck by not believing that this is also meant to be our reality. It is the call of God for you, right here and right now.

EMMA STARK

INTRODUCTION

THERE IS SOMETHING INHERENT IN HUMANS THAT IMPELS US to reach past what is familiar and go into the 'as yet' uncharted space. We are curious about unexplored lands. Whether as tourists or extreme adventurers, each will go where very few dare. We all have a part within us that longs to experience the new, whether in person or from our armchairs! When we watch human effort focus on discovering the depths and breadth of the world's oceans, we may picture ourselves in scuba gear. We celebrate human feats of ascending the highest mountains and we track exploration missions into the deep unknown of space. Technology enables what was previously impossible to become possible; to move beyond what we thought were the boundaries and to alter what we once thought was firm, immoveable and real.

What are we being called to explore? What can we see that we have not yet seen? What might we experience that is currently out of reach?

We humans have been intrigued by the hidden realms for centuries. From the oceans beneath the earth itself to star gazing and space exploration, our question is focused on what *is* out there? We even push beyond into another dimension and wonder: Are angels real? Are there such things as visible spirits? Literature, poetry and film explore these questions over centuries: Is there life beyond our earth realm? Is there something hidden beyond what we can see?

Literary classics such as *Alice in Wonderland*, an 1865 novel by English author Lewis Carroll, or *The Secret Garden* by American writer Frances Hodgson Burnett, first published in 1911, still capture the imagination of our children today. These stories provoke us to explore hidden worlds where lives and destinies are fulfilled and dreams come true—worlds where anything is possible and realities are transformed through human interaction.

Movies like *The Matrix* and sci-fi classic *Star Trek* push the boundaries of what is or isn't fact. They urge us to think beyond our experience: 'to go where no man has gone before.'

'Space: the final frontier. These are the voyages of the Starship Enterprise. Its five-year mission: to explore strange new worlds, to seek out new life and new civilizations…to boldly go where no man has gone before!' This pioneering thought is sealed by the iconic quote from Captain James T. Kirk. However, the phrase originally comes from the journal of Captain James Cook, the famous 18th-century explorer of new worlds and an expert cartographer. He found and mapped Australia, New Zealand, Hawaii and more—places that for many people from his world did not even exist.

Yet Captain Cook had the desire, expertise, focus and drive to go beyond all previously set geographic and human boundaries. As a pioneer explorer, he went outside the parameters of what was accepted, driven to discover *if* there was more. That drive moved him to discover and chart new territories so others could find them too.

So what if there is even more? More beyond what we know and is familiar to us and the solidity of the earth we live on? Our inner explorer is inquisitive at that thought. We could go wild at the innumerable possibilities. Conspiracies abound as to what is true and what is only the dust of imagination.

What if there is something beyond the reality we can see with our natural eyes; something beyond the recognisable that we are accustomed to and something, both within reach and at hand, that we have not fully grasped? *The realm of the spirit.* This unseen and uncharted territory is something real and yet undiscovered by many. Our eyes and senses can be opened to this invisible realm, which is as real as the one we inhabit—a realm that a great spiritual leader told us to prioritise above what we currently see. Apostle Paul writes in Second Corinthians 4:18:

> *So we fix our eyes not on what is seen, but on what is unseen, since what is seen is temporary, but what is unseen is eternal.*

We need eyes on the everlasting created order, the eternal perspective. We must be focused and look beyond what is here now before us—fixing rather on the unseen. Let us experience—as we look and see with all our senses blazing—a new, previously invisible, unknown world that is and always has been right before our eyes. A world at hand with access at our fingertips.

We are now in the era of the 'Great Watch of the Lord'. The invitation has come from Him to, "Watch and look with Me." We need to be the ones who have eyes to see and ears to hear the remarkable hidden mysteries that are in this concealed yet accessible Kingdom. There is a world available now to all those who are born again.

This invitation is to see beyond and experience more than we ever have previously. A new paradigm will bring the Word of God alive to us in mind-blowing, life-shaping and remarkable ways. Spiritual realities will manifest through God's people supernaturally. There is an unseen created order to be experienced. We can immerse our senses in what brings transformation to us and those around us.

Are you ready to be born again, to see and go beyond together and to experience this new unseen realm? You are invited and so welcome.

PRAYER

Lord God, in the name of Jesus Christ, I hear the call of the pioneer and explorer and say yes to adventuring with You into the previously unknown and unseen places. I say yes to going on this journey with my senses trained to be fixed on the unseen, invisible realm. To be one awakened to You, Your Word and Your Kingdom in a new way. I say yes to You and give You full access to me, to all of my senses, knowing that all You have for me is good and perfect in Your will and Your timing. Lead me in the way everlasting and enable me to see beyond with You. Amen.

SEEING IS BELIEVING

Jesus Christ had been my Saviour for around ten years.

I was lying on the floor of a church building during the worship time, overwhelmed with emotion. As the music continued to play, I was overcome, both with my love for Jesus and the tangible presence of God. I remember I was crying, not pretty little tears, but snotty, messy wet-face tears. I was embarrassed at the outburst of my emotion to such a degree that I had covered my face with my arm; and yet I couldn't stop.

My thoughts were on the theme of: *I know You love me, Jesus, but I want more! I love You, Jesus, but I want to love You more!* It was burning inside me…a provocation to more hunger, more burning adoration.

In a single moment, I saw Jesus. He was right there; and I saw Him with my eyes open. Yet He was not in solid form. Even though He looked like a man, His form was more like light with a hologram/projected effect. Nevertheless, He was actually present in that moment. I saw Him. His eyes were filled with light and adoration. I heard His voice and I experienced His presence tangibly. It was an 'other worldly' encounter, but it was not ethereal to the point of being unreachable. This was really happening, and Jesus was really there.

He sat in front of me. With His face coming closer to mine, He reached over and kissed me on the cheek. I felt the determined touch. I was still on the floor in more puddles of tears as I experienced the overwhelming adoration and passion of Jesus for me flooding through my body. I can still feel where He kissed me on my face as I write this today.

I heard Him say, 'Let Me hold you now.' He lay next to me. Putting his arm under my head, He pulled me to Him and just held me. It seemed the longest time passed, but it was probably only minutes. I wept as His profound, tangible love filled me like waves, over and over again. I had known His love before, but not like this. This was deep and it transcended everything else that had come before. This was burning adoration from Jesus to me and back again. There was no question about His love for me.

Let him kiss me with the kisses of his mouth—for your love is more delightful than wine (Song of Songs 1:2).

It was not a vision; it was not a dream. I was fully alert and awake. I could see and sense that Jesus was really present in that moment. I was encountering Him in the convergence of the unseen spirit realm and in the seen realm where I physically was. I was transformed in that moment and never the same again. The reality of Christ's devotion settled on me in a moment. He loved me and I loved Him. It was sealed.

This place of reality, where what is hidden in the spirit realm breaks through into the natural earthly realm we inhabit, is something I now experience daily. Seeing, hearing and feeling with all the natural senses in their spiritual mode. This experience can be yours too.

Spirit Realm Reality

Spirit realm reality is more real than our day-to-day lives. More alive and impactful. This coexistence of life and experience is beyond the boundaries of the known world. It is not found in exploration of new geographic territories or through gaining more knowledge with developing thought. This amazing new world of discovery is found right in front of us. It is right beside us if we can but see it.

Stretch out your hand, focus your eyes and see. The invitation is open and access is available to you. Experience the unseen realm with me. This concealed realm is of the spirit: unseen and yet accessible with ease as we focus on it and focus on its King, Jesus Christ.

SEEK FIRST THE KINGDOM! SEEK MY FACE!

As we seek the Kingdom and His face, what was once beyond our limits and borders of 'known' and 'explored' territory is suddenly exposed as false. We begin to see that our 'here and now reality' is greater than what exists in front of us. Reality is multi-layered. This glorious hidden Kingdom can be more than seen; fullness of encounter and deep connection bring our relationship with God and understanding of His Word more fully alive.

Interaction with the unseen place allows us to work with the Spirit of God in a way which enables our 'seen' realm to be transformed. Through Christ there is an open door of access to the realms of the spirit where God Himself resides. The fantastical world we read of in the Word of God becomes our new realism and actuality. Let us explore this new unseen reality together and allow our curiosity to be provoked and stirred. Let us desire to know Jesus and God the Father more. Let us wait for the door to open for full access.

LOOK AND WATCH

When we look at the view in front of us—perhaps a picturesque scene, our own garden or a city park—we begin to gaze. Our senses quieten as our internal world stills under our focus. We hear more—the breeze, the birds, the children playing far off, splashes of the water nearby, perhaps an airplane overhead. We are aware of our own breathing, the comfort from the warmth of the sunshine on our face or the fresh crisp air of the winter, depending on the season.

As we gaze, we begin to see what is actually before us. The details emerge in the scene in front of us, details we had not seen before: the shadows the sun casts; shapes we had not previously perceived. Our peripheral vision and senses become aware of the breadth of the images, sounds and feelings around us. As we watch in the stillness, a new world view appears before our eyes. As we gaze, we sense and see that which we never would have if we hadn't paused.

Watching and seeing in the spirit realm has a similar principle to this. It comes to many of us in places of natural beauty. It requires internal stillness and our gaze fixed in one place. As we do this, we begin to feel and see the previously hidden realm emerging. It is as if it appears out of the background of what we are looking at.

In a similar way, we may look at a familiar Old Master's artwork. We see a 'snapshot' because we have glanced at the image. We have not seen the multifaceted, multi-layered meaning and experienced a personal response. However, in the gazing and in the focus, we begin to see more; we see and sense a new depth.

SEEK FIRST

I believe that the sight and sense of that which is in the spirit realm is available and accessible to all. I also know that it is crucial to access the hidden 'realm at hand' through Jesus Christ and no other. This brings us through and into 'the light of life' that is Christ. This keeps us safe. In Christ, we have all authority in His name and through the power of His blood. We remain 'hidden in Him' as we begin to see and sense that which was previously hidden from us.

If there is a hunger in you for more of Jesus and more of the Father, if your yearning is to know God both individually and as the Trinity, then please keep reading. To engage fully with the Lord and the realm of the spirit He abides in, our internal gaze and desire needs to be fixed on Jesus and His Kingdom. We need to hunger for the fullness of experience and encounter the life in Christ available to us now.

My heart says of you, 'Seek his face!' Your face, Lord, I will seek (Psalm 27:8).

But seek first his kingdom and his righteousness, and all these things will be given to you as well (Matthew 6:33).

If we follow these two commands given to us in Scripture, we will always be focused on the Lord. If our worship, our adoration, our internal heart posture is submitted to Him daily, we will always be in the optimum place for encounter and experience. We will be perfectly positioned to leave our natural senses open to the spirit.

When we open our eyes to seeing the reality of the previously hidden sights of the heavenly realms, to Jesus Himself, the angels, the vast expanses of the 'unseen spheres of the heavens', we open ourselves to so much more. Once we have allowed our senses to be awakened to the sights, smells, sounds and feelings of the heavenly realms, we waken a fresh and new hunger for more.

Blessed are those who hunger and thirst for righteousness, for they will be filled (Matthew 5:6).

Let us allow ourselves to be hungry for more, so that we may be filled. Move beyond uncertainty and even perhaps fear of what is 'out there'. When we begin with Jesus Christ and focus on Him, we only see and experience what He wants us to. We only go where He gives us access. We go in His timing and in His way.

I SAW JESUS

The first time I saw Jesus in the spirit was during a prayer ministry training I was attending at my local church. He walked into the room with His arms wide, dressed in a loose-fitting white robe. He stood there for some time, an open, warm expression on His face: I felt in that moment He was saying to all of us in the room, 'I am easily accessible.'

I had prayed for some years that God would 'open the eyes of my heart' and that I would know Him more. My driver was not actually to see and sense in the spirit—although I would have loved that—but more to understand and to better know God and His ways, to have His wisdom in my life. In that prayer, God opened my spiritual senses fully. He bestowed on me the precious gift of interacting with that which is hidden, of lifting the veil between the seen and unseen realms.

My prayer was simple—the same prayer King Solomon prayed—that of heart illumination. This was God's wisdom from Ephesians 1—make this your prayer also and be prepared to go on the journey of having your spiritual senses come alive in Christ.

Your Response

Allow your heart and senses to be awakened to seek God: to see the face of Jesus Christ, to desire to know God and understand Him more. I pray for the spirit of wisdom and revelation of God the Most High to be yours today and going forward, increasing in and through you for God's own glory.

> *I have not stopped giving thanks for you, remembering you in my prayers, that the God of our Lord Jesus Christ, the glorious Father, may give you a spirit of wisdom and revelation in your knowledge of Him. I ask that the eyes of your heart may be enlightened, so*

that you may know the hope of His calling, the riches of His glorious inheritance in the saints, and the surpassing greatness of His power to us who believe... (Ephesians 1:16-19 BSB).

I pray, as you meditate on these verses, that God will open the eyes of your heart to see and know Him and to receive His wisdom. I pray for you to gain greater understanding of God and His ways as He opens your heart to see with clarity.

PRAYER

If you can, please lay your hand on your heart and pray the following over yourself:

Lord God, I give You the fullness of my heart in the name of Jesus Christ. Lord, I ask that You open the eyes of my heart so I may know You more. I ask for the spirit of wisdom and revelation to fall upon me now in accordance with Ephesians 1:17–18 and awaken my senses to You and the ways of Your Kingdom. Lord, I give You all of my senses: my eyes to see; my ears to hear; my emotions and touch to feel; my nose and mouth to smell and taste.

You may wish to lay your hands on each part of your body mentioned in the prayer as you pray each one in turn and apply your will, choosing to give the Lord your senses. Take time over this. I pray you and your senses are now awakened to the living God in a greater way and that you begin to sense, to see and hear God more.

PRAYER

Lord, I submit my senses fully to You now. Speak Lord, I am listening. Open the eyes of my heart that I may see You and know You more.

ACTION

Following this prayer, ask the Holy Spirit to bring to mind anything you might have watched, seen or heard that has clouded or diminished your senses. It could be a book, a film or even something in your life that is etched on your memory and causes an unhelpful filter.

I urge you to take time with the Holy Spirit and ask, 'Is there anything affecting my senses as I submit them to You that You want to alert me to now, Lord?' Take time to listen before Him. Write down what you hear or what is being brought to mind. I encourage you not to attempt to recall a memory with your thinking but to allow the Holy Spirit to move sovereignly here.

If nothing is there, that is wonderful! Please don't go digging! If a situation or memory is accessed by the Holy Spirit, bring it back in prayer. If you feel convicted, ask for forgiveness for your part in watching/hearing what you did. Ask for the Holy Spirit to cleanse the memory of that from you and cleanse your senses of the memory.

If anything the Holy Spirit has brought to mind is affecting the clarity of your senses, then ask Him what to do with them. If there are, for example, films/books of a violent, horror or highly sexual nature, my sense would be that it is time to remove them from your home, your computer or your bookshelf. If there are items that remind you of difficult historic events in your family or your personal life, this may be the time to store them away. However, if you are highly triggered by them, perhaps ask a family member or friend to hold them for you. You may want to see these items again once God has brought complete healing. To see and sense clearly, we need to have pure sight and guard our sense 'gates' from experiencing anything that has the potential to cloud our minds.

Now, I pray for you that, as you action what the Holy Spirit has highlighted in you, you will rest well knowing that God has you and all these people and issues in His hands. Trust Him with His timing. Trust His ways of caring for all that is associated with this journey of exploration and the adventure of knowing God more.

SEEING JESUS ACTIVATION

The first place and Person we should desire to see and encounter is always Jesus Christ. I recommend that you look for Him and seek His face daily. Set your heart and your internal gaze on Him alone. Ensure that you are set right, that your internal compass and focus is upon Him first and always.

A helpful activation is to be able to sense and see Jesus for yourself, in a way similar to the experience I shared with you earlier in this chapter. I encourage you, daily if possible, to take time to be in the presence of Jesus.

Find a quiet place and sit with your eyes closed. It may help to have instrumental worship music in the background. Focus your being on Jesus and ask, 'Where are You right now, Jesus?' You are not thinking Jesus is seated at the right hand of the Father in this moment; rather, is Jesus in proximity to *you* right now? Is He in the physical place where you are? If He is in the corner of the room or space where you are, invite Him closer, to come right next to you. The purpose of the invitation is to be comfortable having Jesus next to you, touching you, allowing Him to speak to you and minister to you there.

What is Jesus wearing? What does He look like? Is He in His transcendent form or is He revealing Himself as the man, Jesus Christ from Nazareth, who walked on the earth as the Rabbi, the Healer or something else of His character and form? There are many ways you will encounter Jesus the more you practise this. As He comes to you, ask Him, 'Jesus, what would You like to say to me and for me to know in this moment?' Another question may be, 'What would You like to give me?' Watch and sense what He is doing. Allow Him to minister to you in this moment. Take time. Keep your focus and spend time with Jesus: He has so much He longs to share with you personally.

Regularly taking time with Jesus like this will personally transform you and your perspective. It will bring healing and reset when needed. You will begin the process of opening your senses to the realm of the spirit at the right start and focal point. It is all about Jesus after all.

Pause here and take time with Jesus before moving on to the next chapter. Close your eyes and encounter Him. Let Him speak to you and minister in the way He desires. Receive from Jesus and allow Him to marinate you in His presence.

2

ACCESS ALL AREAS

THERE IS A DIFFERENCE BETWEEN BELIEVING IN GOD AND knowing God. James 2:19 informs us that even the demons believe in God and shudder! We may believe but do we truly 'know' God? The knowledge of God and His Christ moves beyond memorizing Scripture, talking to God and praying with our requests to Him. Of course, it is absolutely vital to read, to meditate on and to know Scripture; however, our God, who is One, Jesus Christ, is not some historic figure who is distanced from how we live today. The 'knowledge of God' comes from us experiencing the living Word Himself. The Word is made flesh in this epoch of time as we live out our daily lives.

This 'knowledge' comes through knowing fully the Christ who is resurrected and seated at the right hand of the Father today: through knowing that the Holy Spirit is alive on earth, advocating for us and teaching us in the ways of God; of knowing and experiencing the love of the Father as His arms open to us today. The 'knowledge of God' comes from spending time with the Persons of God—our God, the Trinity, who is three in one:

> *Hear, O Israel: the Lord our God, the Lord is one* (Deuteronomy 6:4).

I saw God the Father, Jesus Christ the Son and the Holy Spirit together in the spiritual realm watching over the earth recently, their attention focused on the British Isles. They were sitting together, watching from the unseen realm and concentrating on the land mass and seas around the islands. They were watching in the spirit and agreeing together as They looked.

I could see that the glory of God, in all its brilliance of illuminating light, was tangibly focused on the British Isles. More than 6,000 islands of land together encompass England, Ireland, Scotland and Wales, each with its own diverse beauty and culture but 'as one' in this moment, covered in the deep golden hues of God's glory. The Godhead was discussing the British Isles together, agreeing and speaking as one. They were saying together, 'It is time!' Time for the renewed transformation of the British Isles to commence in this era.

In the Gregorian calendar this was just before the United Kingdom's government permanently left the European Union Parliament at the end of 2020. As our Three-in-One God spoke, there was, at that moment, a sense that this was a new beginning at that specific point in time.

Why does God allow us to see and witness what He is doing in any given moment on the earth or in the heavens as in this case?

Amos 3:7 says, *"Surely the Sovereign Lord does nothing* [in other translations "no good thing"] *without revealing his plan to his servants the prophets."*

God grants us access to see what He is doing through this scriptural principle. God has chosen to involve us individually as citizens of Heaven on earth. He invites us to participate as those who 'co-labour' with God, the concept Paul explains in First Corinthians 3. Yes, God moves sovereignly and mysteriously. He does not require us to do something to enable Him to be God, yet He does invite us to participate in what He is doing and hear what He is saying when He chooses.

Knowing God more involves seeing and experiencing the living Word of God as He speaks it and as it is released. Feeling and experiencing the moments when God is moving on earth and in the heavens is an incredible privilege and joy. We can also experience the intense fear of the Lord as we hear and observe. It can be extremely difficult and emotionally challenging if what God reveals to us is painful or gruelling. There have often been occasions when I have been laughing and filled with joy at what the Lord has revealed, alongside weeping in grief or fear and awe of Him and His ways.

We see repeatedly in Scripture how prophets like Daniel and Ezekiel are overcome, incapacitated even, by what they encountered. We see what they witnessed in the spirit realm as God chose to open wisdom and revelation to them. When the prophet Ezekiel encountered the cherubim, the holy fire, the powerful wheels with eyes all around and the Lord Himself burning brightly and intensely, seated on the throne, he received a word from the Lord that laid heavily upon him. As God spoke to him, Ezekiel was weighed down with the full impact of the revelation he had been given. (See Ezekiel, chapter 1.) He could not recover in that moment.

> *The Spirit then lifted me up and took me away, and I went in bitterness and in the anger of my spirit, with the strong hand of the Lord on me. I came to the exiles who lived at Tel Aviv near the River Kebar. And there, where they were living, I sat among them for seven days—deeply distressed* (Ezekiel 3:14-15).

Ezekiel is in a geographical location, with the exiles of Israel after they have been taken captive by the Babylonians. In this place of uncertainty and captivity, God speaks to His prophet. The spirit realm opened before Ezekiel's eyes and the Lord brought His word through Ezekiel to His people, Israel. Expect the spirit realm to open to you in your geographical location at any time God chooses to reveal something to you. I encourage you to read Ezekiel chapters 1–3 (ideally read the full Book of Ezekiel) to understand both the completeness of the revelation God releases to the prophets and their experience. As you read, ask the Lord to show you what He desires you to experience from the knowledge of Scripture and the revelation from the Spirit of God.

Are we all prophets? No. The office of prophet, in accordance with Ephesians 2, is reserved for those God chooses to give their lives to that call. However, each person who will read this book, including you, has the ability to hear the voice of God and see what He wants to reveal to you. Perhaps not initially in the same full-blown detail Ezekiel had, yet I know many people who have awakened spiritual senses in a moment. They experience being 'fully loaded' immediately with smells, feeling and sounds. Others go on a slower journey of awakening. Either way, you have this capacity in you because of Christ in you. The passage to your spiritual senses awakening is personal and bespoke to you as God reveals Himself and His story through your life. You are unique, and your spiritual senses' awakening story will be unique to you.

> *My sheep listen to my voice; I know them, and they follow me* (John 10:27).

We hear and know the voice of God and He knows us individually. This is indisputable if you have heard the call to follow Jesus Christ and said yes. The other truth we must recognise and receive is that the word of God speaks to all who are in Christ.

> *For you can all prophesy in turn so that everyone may be instructed and encouraged* (1 Corinthians 14:31).

The gift of prophecy is the ability to hear and sense what God is saying and then to speak out that understanding from the revelation we are given. If we take both scriptural truths together, we can hear and sense in the spirit what God is saying. We hear and know His voice *and* we can tell others of the revelation from God through His Spirit's unction. All born-again believers can prophesy.

Realms of Sensing

There are a number of locations from where we can receive revelation. We should be ready in any place on earth at any given time. Revelation may come where you are now standing or sitting; it may come in the street or on the hilltop, just as we read earlier about Ezekiel's revelation. We can deliberately be seeking the Lord in that precise moment and the spirit realm opens. If you practise seeking out the Lord daily, the realm of the spirit can open at any time. Be expectant as you go through your everyday life!

My prayer for you is to posture yourself to be hungry to know God more and to know His ways more (see Psalm 86:11). Make this your focus and prayer and the Lord will hear, respond and open your senses. You will encounter Him in fresh and deeply life-transforming ways—all aimed at bringing you closer to Him and to an understanding and knowledge of Him.

I pray for your senses to be awakened, to be defibrillated and shocked by the Spirit of God!

THREE GOD ENCOUNTERS

God did exactly this to me through a series of three encounters within a few months of each other. I was walking in the city—twice in Glasgow, Scotland, and once in London—when it happened. On these occasions, I was busy, hurrying on my way somewhere. I was not intentionally praying for revelation in those moments but—I believe that it was because I had cultivated a lifestyle of prayer and focus on God at all times—He 'broke in' to open my eyes intentionally in order to teach me something.

Each time this occurred, everything I saw in front of me—for example, people walking towards me, just going about their business—was in slow motion. It was bizarre and yet similar to a movie scene in slow motion and then changing to three dimensional for a few minutes.

The first time, in a split second, I began to see all the 'spiritual clothes' each person was wearing. As they walked by, I could see that all of the 'clothes' had words written on them such as lust, greed, depression and fear. I could see the clothing as well as feel and hear it in the spirit. God revealed that the sounds of these clothes were from the spirits they were associated with. Fear was the loudest, most high pitched, dreadful screeching sound of them all. This 'clothing' can travel great distances in the spirit, with fear travelling the furthest. With the revelation came the realisation that any demonic spirit or person operating in spiritual sight could easily see and sense what everyone of us had partnered with—unintentionally or otherwise.

The second occasion the Lord opened my spiritual senses was when I was walking through a busy train station. The slow-motion experience occurred again, but this time I could see 'through' people's bodies, much like a supernatural x-ray. I saw internal organs lit up in different colours— black for diseased hearts and kidneys; green where healing was coming to other body parts; thyroid and endocrine functions and more. As God spoke, my eyes were led to what was wrong health-wise with each person.

The final time this 'defibrillation' occurred, again I was not intentionally seeking God or training my spiritual senses. However, I immediately saw demonic, scorpion-like creatures appear on the backs of the individuals in front of me. These spiritual 'creatures' were secured to people's shoulders. Their tail-like appendages were fastened on to the spine like a macabre backpack. Not every person had these creatures on them. God showed me that these creatures represented demonic strongholds which had attached themselves through great agency and agreement from the individuals carrying them. The gift of the discernment of spirits from First Corinthians 12 enabled me to know what they were.

After this, I knew I could train my senses on to people and see and feel where the illness was in a body; I could perceive which spirit a person was wearing or carrying, just as God had shown me in these encounters.

Unsurprisingly, it took me some time to overcome the initial amazement of seeing inside bodies, to overcome the horror at seeing the demonic so clearly visible on people. Truthfully, it briefly became an unhealthy focus until I took it to the Lord. I knew I could become wrongly obsessed with the demonic if I were not careful. I needed to re-set my gaze on the Lord and ask how He wanted me to use this amazing gift I had been given.

My response to the visible demonic pushed me away from rather than towards these people and thus away from offering help. In the early days of God opening my spiritual senses, I struggled at times with what God was revealing to me. I would even say that I wrestled with the Lord over why He had decided to show me these things. Eventually I realised what a blessing this gift was and is. Truly it is a remarkable gift.

Working through the challenges enabled a drawing closer to God. I began to be able to pray with people and see and feel what illness or spirit was at work in their lives. I was able to ask the Lord for the solution through His Spirit to bring freedom and/or healing as I ministered to them. It is an incredible gift to see and sense in the Spirit the demonic shift and divine healing come to individuals repeatedly.

I believe this awakening and opening of our senses is available to all of us in Christ Jesus. It is open for you to access today.

DISCERNMENT OF SPIRITS

The Lord longs for us to be those 'born of the spirit' who realise all that He has gifted us: to experience and interact within the unseen realms at any point in time as He desires to open it to us. The Lord longs to show you where you may be stuck or in difficulty due to a demonic spirit or spirits at work.

My daughter Sophie was at primary school when she experienced difficulties with a child in her class, one who made life at school so challenging that Sophie no longer wanted to attend school.

35

God spoke and told me to ask Sophie to look in the spirit and see what demons were working through the child at school. This would show her there were unseen spirits causing the issue. As we did this exercise together, the Lord opened Sophie's eyes and showed her two demonic spirits. I asked her to draw them and write the names on them that God told her. She did this with ease as, from a young age, she was used to seeing and sensing in the spirit.

When Sophie completed the drawing and naming, we prayed it through together. It immediately made her feel better that she could see what was against her was spirit, not flesh and blood. Sophie then had great compassion for the child. The next day, without any further intervention from me, I received a phone call from the head teacher to tell me that the child was being moved into another class. What an amazing testimony that was for Sophie.

What difficulty are you having right now? Ask the Lord to shine His illuminating light on it. Ask to see the spirit(s) at work 'behind the scenes' of the natural. Look beyond your circumstance into the spirit realm. God will surely reveal it to you. You may not get an image, but you may have a strong sense and feeling of what they are and what their role is in disrupting your life.

Perhaps you are being overlooked for promotion or experiencing great challenges in relationships. You know what it is. Seek out the Lord intentionally, with focus but without panic and He will reveal it to you.

To be effective in this area of discernment, we must operate in the gift of the discernment of spirits. If this is novel to you, read First Corinthians 12 again. In verse 10 we read about the 'distinguishing' or 'discerning' of spirits. With this gift from Holy Spirit, we may understand every spirit at work in a situation, in our own or another person's life, at any point in time. The different spirits are:

- Human—Our own driver that causes us to feel and act in certain ways (Psalm 43:5)
- Demonic—The numerous spirits who work with satan to interfere with our God-given destiny
- Holy—The Holy Spirit Himself at work in and through us and in various situations and circumstances

So which is it? Ask yourself, 'Is the current delay I am facing due to my own reluctance and/or doubt in myself?' Is it human or demonic interference saying, 'You can't have this', or even the Holy Spirit's intervention saying, 'I am closing this door' or 'This is not My timing for you, wait'? The only way we discover which it is, is through practising the gift of discernment of spirits and seeking the Lord. Let us not be reluctant discerners or revelators; rather let us press into the spiritual training!

PRAYER

You can begin with a prayer like this:

Holy Spirit, I ask You in the name of Jesus Christ to activate in me the gift of discerning between spirits, that I may understand the spirits at work in my life and understand Your ways more. Lord, I long to be in time with You and move with You always. Teach me the way of discernment that I may have Your wisdom in personal life choices and help others.

I pray for you now: an impartation of the gift to activate and kick start your journey of exercising and practising this amazing gift muscle, to know and understand the ways of the spirit realm more, how they affect your life and others you love and care about, to see and sense the different spirits at work and learn their nuances and, finally, to understand what to do as these are revealed to you.

This gift of discernment is essential for any form of spiritual warfare—deliverance or strategic prayer on land, for regions or nations. We must know first which spirit is at work. Then, from the gifts of wisdom, prophecy and knowledge, we will understand the strategy from the Lord to bring healing and freedom from the person, group, organisation or even the land. This gift is crucial for us to be effective advancers of the Kingdom of God. For example, if we are trying to bring deliverance from a spirit when we are dealing with human pain, then without this gift of discernment, we could make the person much worse off than before we began.

Cultivate this gift and practise it. You will find that with exercise you will come to know instinctively what spirit is at work and how to pray. Be encouraged that you have been given this gift. Our job is to activate and practise this gift until we become mature in it!

INTO HEAVEN

In addition to earth's realm where we live, God also gives us the ability to see and sense into the heavens. Apostle Paul tells us:

> *I must go on boasting. Although there is nothing to be gained, I will go on to visions and revelations from the Lord. I know a man in Christ who fourteen years ago was caught up to the third heaven. Whether it was in the body or out of the body I do not know—God knows. And I know that this man—whether in the body or apart from the body I do not know, but God knows—was caught up to paradise and heard inexpressible things, things that no one is permitted to tell* (2 Corinthians 12:1-4).

Paul is expressing the mystery of encountering God. With his and others' experience, he knows of being *'caught up to the third heaven'*, the place Bible scholars understand to be the place of God's throne and where the legions of angels reside. 'The heavens' as described in Scripture, denote the realms between earth and the third heaven. The first heaven is the atmosphere surrounding the earth, the second heaven is where the stars, planets and galaxies are located and the third heaven is where God resides, in Heaven. All of these areas in the created and unseen realm of the spirit are accessible and open to us through Christ Jesus.

When Jesus says in Matthew 3 that *'the kingdom of heaven is at hand'*, He means full access to the realm of the Kingdom of God is within our reach—not thousands of light years or thousands of earth miles, but right here at your hand. Imagine your hand has a spiritual knife in it, one that can cut through this 'earth realm' where we see with our natural eyes and feel with our natural senses, a knife that can cut through to the previously unseen spiritual realm. In this way, we ourselves can 'cut through' to see what is in the spirit here, what is happening in the spirit and from the spirit realm back to earth.

The original Hebrew pictorial symbol for one who is a 'seer' in the spirit is the scythe, and with it the tent image denoting the veil between the earth and the cosmos, what we call the stratosphere. In effect, when we see through to the invisible realm, we are cutting through and revealing what was previously hidden.

I, and many other seers I know, can easily see and sense from the realm of the cosmos—what we call 'space', from a position looking back at the earth. Many times God speaks about the nations and what He is doing from this viewpoint in the cosmos. In addition, we can be caught up, like John in Revelation 4, to see and sense in the third heaven, deep into the spirit where God in His mystery resides, where He discloses more about Himself and His ways.

Should we always reference the Bible to see if our encounters and experiences can be explained through the Word of God? *Yes!* Absolutely. Always. We never allow ourselves to be deceived intentionally. We know Scripture warns us to be careful about deception and that even the faithful are open to it. In these days especially we are aware of the enemy's assignment to release deception and confusion. We need to be the ones who study and wash our minds in the Word of God daily. We do not want to be those who go off track, who get lost in the realm of the spirit without being anchored in the Word of God.

But solid food is for the mature, who by constant use have trained themselves to distinguish good from evil (Hebrews 5:14).

I will explain how to ensure we all keep ourselves closed off to deception in later chapters. For now, I would like to give you a specific prayer. As you are learning to open yourself and your senses more, this prayer will help to throw a protective shield around you and your encounters as you practise exercising your senses further. If we crave to be those with mature spiritual senses, we must intentionally focus as we exercise them. We must not be wary of entering, but we should be wise. Going carefully and submitting to our spiritual director and/or spiritual leader with our encounters and experiences will help us to remain sharp and on point with Scripture.

PRAYER

God, in the name of the Lord Jesus Christ, I pray that You awaken my senses more, day by day and night by night; but I say, Lord, let me see and sense nothing but the Kingdom of God. I desire to know You and You alone, God. I desire to see and sense only that which brings me closer to You. So I say again, nothing but the Kingdom of God may be seen and I will only see and sense that which You wish me to. Thank You, Lord, for training my senses.

I pray that you go out in wisdom and godly caution, not timidity. That you will be bold in experiencing only that which the Lord desires to reveal to you in His own timing. That your desire is always fixed on Jesus Christ and no other. That, from this adoration of Jesus, the Lord Himself will reveal His mysteries and understanding to you in His timing.

DAY AND NIGHT

It may be obvious to say our spiritual senses are also awakened in our sleeping as well as our waking hours. Spiritual revelation from the Lord comes through dreams and night-time encounters that may feel more like visions. I, and many seers I know, dream throughout the night, having multiple dreams that blend into one long series of revelations. God speaks into personal situations. He brings understanding into the areas where we have a calling to be responsible: work; ministry; people; as well as for those who are watchmen in prayer, speaking into their areas of spiritual authority over the regions and nations.

This is not a book about unpacking dreams. There are a number of brilliant and helpful biblical books available for this teaching but it is important for us to know and to expect that God will break into our nights and bring revelation through the activation of our spiritual senses. I recommend reading the Book of Daniel for study on visions and dreams. We see Daniel often interacting within the realm of the spirit and receiving 'night-time revelation'.

I encourage you to study Daniel chapter 7 in particular, where Daniel describes his *'vision at night'* where he is intentionally training his senses throughout. We read here that he *'looked'*, *'watched'* and continued to watch throughout the vision. He then became troubled as he experienced the dream and looked for an interpretation. Approaching *'one of those standing there'* (whom we take to be an angel) gave him the explanation, the interpretation of the dream (Daniel 7:16).

We must become used not only to experiencing the spirit realm but interacting in it as the Lord reveals through Daniel. We are encouraged by Daniel's example not to fear questioning the angels and creatures that we may encounter in the heavenly realms through dreams and visions. He says in different ways that he *'wanted to know about'* such and such (Daniel 7:20) in the vision, so he asked for an explanation. This incredible depth of understanding Daniel gleans from the vision in the dream only comes to him because he is intentionally looking, watching and asking questions. May we be those who ask for understanding like Daniel.

While training many people in seeing and sensing in the spirit over years, I have found that we can often become so overwhelmed and in awe of what we are seeing that we forget to ask, 'What is the meaning of all this, Lord?' The beauty and the incredible things you may see will stretch your mind and capacity for thought! You will often be lost in the vision and the encounter because they can be so incredible. The display of other worldly and often hugely emotional beauty is intense.

I urge you, friend, do not forget to ask: 'Why are You showing me this, Lord? What do You want me to know from this vision? What are You allowing me to see and/or sense, Lord?' Knowing the answers to these questions ensures that you receive the full understanding you are longing for. Don't let it just be an amazing dream or vision that leaves you thinking, 'Wow, that was incredible!' Come back with more understanding or knowledge than before it happened!

PRAYER

Lord God, as this reader rests and sleeps tonight, I pray for an awakening of senses in the realm of sleep. I pray that this person will be activated in the dream vision realm as Daniel was. That my friend here instinctively knows in the dream to ask and to interact in the moment as You reveal Your great mysteries, Lord, through Your dream language.

3

TASTE AND SEE

FULLY LOADED MEANS ALL SENSES ARE ALIVE—SMELLING, hearing, tasting, seeing and feeling—everything in the unseen realm is possible for all those who are born again in Christ. We are spirit beings inside a physical body. We are connected in the spirit to the living God, making us one with Him. We are one in spirit and therefore have full access through Jesus Christ.

> *But whoever is united with the Lord is one with him in spirit* (1 Corinthians 6:17).

Without all our natural senses alive and working we would have only a partial experience of what the world has to offer us. If our smell or taste falters, we cannot enjoy all that is beautiful and delicious! If we are diminished in our natural sight, we learn to 'see' with our other senses. We are, however, poorer for not seeing with our eyes all the colours and scenes in daily life. The amazing phenomena of the world's natural beauty is diminished.

This is also true of our spiritual senses. Without them all fully operating our revelation can be diminished.

We see in apostle John's experience in Revelation 4 that without our fully awakened and alive senses in the spirit we would not have the astonishing Scripture verses that communicate the powerful majesty of King Jesus. I encourage you to read this emotive portion of Scripture for yourself again. The way John receives the completeness of revelation from the Lord is what I call the 'turn and look' principle. We read of John hearing the voice of God, then turning and looking at the place God's voice came from! This principle brings the richness and extent of the revelation from the Lord.

Sometimes, in a split second, we might see a flash, a movement or a light from the corner of our spiritual eyes; perhaps we notice an unusual scent in our nostrils. We need to pay attention to these moments because our spiritual senses can be randomly caught. It is then we need to pause, to turn and focus on what caught our attention so we may obtain the complete revelation God is opening to us. If we disregard these twinkling flashes of revelation, we will miss the full picture. It may be fleeting—a scent, a sound, a nudge or knowing—so we must quickly press in and turn our focus to what has 'interrupted' us. We must be ready to wonder, 'What was that?'

Let us focus more fully on the Book of Revelation. In Revelation 1:10-11 we read that apostle John received prophetic words from the Lord when he was *in the Spirit* already, and then he heard a voice instructing him to *'Write on a scroll what you see....'* Following on from this, John says in verse 12, *'I turned round to see the voice that was speaking to me....'* Boom! John decided in an instant to turn and look, to focus his gaze. He turned and saw the voice!

Through his concentration and in fixing his entire gaze on the voice, John revealed one of the most incredible images we read of the unseen realm—an illuminated picture of the seven lampstands and *'someone like the son of man'* and *'His face was like the sun shining in all its brilliance.'* This is the image of Jesus Christ that speaks into generations of Christianity. This is the image that confirms the revelations of Daniel (see Daniel 10), who saw the same *'son of man'* in the spirit realm. The connecting point, seen over hundreds of years, is of the same vision of the Lord with His brilliant, blazing countenance, which is seen and written about repeatedly because John turned and looked at the voice.

What if John had chosen just to *hear* the voice that spoke? Can you imagine not having this incredible image of Jesus Christ imprinted on our souls and spirits from the now into all eternity? The invitation to turn and look is for all of us to notice. Do not disregard the nudges and flashes of breakthrough from the spirit realm. These flash points need to be attended to instantly, to be pressed into so that we gain the fullness of the opening. Let us be the ones who 'open the envelope' of the sense that has been triggered in any given moment and invite *all* our senses to participate.

> *However, as it is written: 'What no eye has seen, what no ear has heard, and what no human mind has conceived'—the things God has prepared for those who love him* (1 Corinthians 2:9).

There is so much more for you to see and experience. God has prepared amazing insight and incredible revelation of

His ways and who He is for you alone. Let us press in for the fullness together.

Some years ago, a person (referred to here as K) we had trained in sensing the spirit was working in a hospital environment and kept smelling rotten fish. K would ask colleagues repeatedly, 'Do you smell that disgusting odour?' No one else did. The realisation came that, due to the training in the senses of the spirit, the likely answer was the smell was emitting from the realm of the spirit, so K pressed into focus on that. In K's concentration of spiritual senses, the spirit of the Lord revealed that the stinking odour was the spirit of death. K was able to gain more revelation once the 'envelope' had been fully opened and understood. K had been suffering in the workplace with great heaviness and a horrible low mood for weeks. Through this odour and with prayer, the Lord illuminated the source of the spirit of death in the workplace. In this way, K gained the advantage through prayer to ensure an easier workday and lighter mood; moreover, it also enabled K to bring prayer with divine wisdom into the atmosphere of the workplace and shift the spirit of death significantly. All from a smell!

Let us be those who go with the nudges and the sense 'alerts'—who knows where God will take you!

Fully Loaded Senses

As we continue to 'train' the spiritual senses into maturity in the Hebrews 5:14 principle, we consider touch and taste. Scripture is full of people who receive revelation through the experience of taste!

Taste and see that the Lord is good... (Psalm 34:8).

We read that the word of God is like tasting honey on the tongue and bitter in the stomach, as it was for the prophets who ate the scrolls: *"Fill your stomach with this", he said. And when I ate it, it tasted as sweet as honey in my mouth'* (Ezekiel 3:3 NLT).

We also learn that there are tastes of fruit from our mouths with breath like apples in Song of Songs 7:8. Experiencing sensations when receiving revelation is to be expected. We read that there can be extreme emotional outpourings as we have seen with Ezekiel 1–4, and specifically Ezekiel 3:15: *'I sat among them for seven days—deeply distressed.'*

In addition, God physically touches and 'marks' His people with a name and symbol as signs of their belonging: *'...put a mark on the foreheads of those who grieve and lament over all the detestable things that are done...'* (Ezekiel 9:4).

> *...and I will also write on them my new name* (Revelation 3:12).

In accordance with Scripture then, when we experience this feeling it can be an emotional or physical tasting revelation. Be ready to taste honey sweetness when reading or receiving insight through revelation from God.

So I went to the angel and asked him to give me the little scroll. He said to me, 'Take it and eat it. It will turn your stomach sour, but "in your mouth it will be as sweet as honey."' I took the little scroll from the angel's hand and ate it. It tasted as sweet as honey in my mouth, but when I had eaten it, my stomach turned sour (Revelation 10:9-10).

Expect, on occasion, that you may have an upset stomach from carrying that revelation. You may have a 'fire in your bones' like Jeremiah in receiving some revelation as all your senses come alive, awakened in and to the spirit (see Jeremiah 20:9 NLT). I have had numerous occasions when I have felt sick in my stomach, overwhelmed emotionally through receipt of revelation. This is normal in Scripture for the prophets. I have felt and heard the rushing of angels' wings both around my body and moving past me.

Equally, you may experience the glorious fragrance of aloes and cassia, the perfume of the King from Psalm 45, or the glorious aroma of sweet roses in the spirit, speaking of love and adoration from Song of Songs 4. Enjoy the revelation coming to you through your senses; it is incredibly powerful.

Personally, I have felt the burning of God and its physical pain. I have been marked by the Spirit over the years. There has been a setting apart in that moment of consecration, a holy burning and consuming in the fire of God. The reality of the unseen spirit realm is present in these moments. It is more than just seeing; it is experiencing the fullness of touch in these powerful times. These experiences are open to you as you allow God to awaken the fullness of your spiritual senses.

The Application of Advancing the Kingdom

When we began as a team from Global Prophetic Alliance (GPA), we were working together to pray and anoint a building which was being repurposed as an outreach café. It had previously been a Chinese restaurant. We were invited by the new, Christian owner who felt it needed to be 'cleansed' spiritually and then dedicated to the Lord. Immediately upon arriving on site, we became aware of the demonic spirits that had made this place their home.

Happy in our teamwork, we gave cleansing and blessing prayers around the building, room by room. When we reached a storeroom at the back of the building, the repugnance we all sensed in the spirit was extraordinary. God revealed to many of us that there had been historic bloodshed in this room. We needed to pray using prophetic acts of salt, water and oil. Salt is used to cleanse and purify (and is also a sign of covenant to and with the Lord), water to wash the land clean (a symbol of the Holy Spirit) and oil to set the space apart for the Lord (showing as it does an element of consecration, anointing and healing). As we did this whilst simultaneously praying, every member of the team saw actual green sulphurous smoke—not only in the spirit, but physically manifested for us to see with our eyes in the natural! We were all completely shocked.

Because I was praying over the location where the salt was thrown, I unintentionally breathed in the smoke. The fumes caused a horrible bout of coughing and was possibly one of the most unpleasant physical experiences of my life at that time.

When we were confident that the building had been cleansed and dedicated to the living God in Jesus' name, we left the venue for our team debrief. It was then we realised the bitter, disagreeable aftertaste in my mouth from this 'demonic smoke' had left an actual, physical mark on my tongue. Dubbed 'demon tongue burn' by us from then on, it appeared the manifested smoke had left what looked like black bruises, clearly visible, on either side of my tongue. It was not painful, but my tongue tasted unpleasant. After much prodding and inspection with a teaspoon, Emma Stark, our leader, decided we would see how it was in the morning and speak then.

I awoke the next day to find my tongue remained black but the taste was slightly less awful. As we discussed over the phone together what the solution might be, we summated that it was a prophetic act that caused the burn. The decision was taken to anoint my tongue with oil, to pray and see what happened! I actually did this whilst we were on the phone together. (I always keep anointing oil at home and in every bag because I never know when I might need it!) While Emma s prayed and as the oil simultaneously touched my tongue, the black marks completely disappeared before my eyes! It was incredible. We all learned in that moment the reality of breaking through from the spirit realm into the natural—*and* not to stand over the place you are cleansing with salt in future!

WE GIVE YOU ALL OUR SENSES

It is time to give your senses to the Lord and become fully alive and loaded in experiencing the realm of the spirit and the completeness of revelation. As you offer this prayer to the Father, you may wish prophetically to touch your senses.

PRAYER

Holy Spirit, in the name of Jesus Christ I give You access to all of my senses: I give You my eyes in the natural and the eyes of my heart and say, 'Open my eyes, Lord.' Lord, I say, consecrate my mouth and tongue to be supersensitised to the Spirit. Awaken me to all that You wish to reveal of the realm of the spirit in tasting Your word. Have my sense of smell, Lord; I give You my nose and its ability to smell. I long to experience the fragrances of Heaven. Open my ears Lord, that I might hear Your voice and the activity in the spirit realm more as You choose to speak to me. I long to feel You, Lord, and touch all that You open to me in the spirit realm. I say, Lord, please activate my sense of touch to You today.

As you pray for yourself and give your senses to the Lord, I say 'Amen' for you to come fully alive in Christ, in all your natural and spiritual senses. Together, we pray this is always with the aim and goal of knowing You, God, and Your ways more; rejoicing always in our salvation and knowing we have access through Jesus Christ to the Kingdom of God today. Thank You, Lord Jesus.

4

LAY DOWN YOUR LIFE

THERE IS AN INVITATION TO GO DEEPER WITH THE LORD THAN you have ever been before. There is a heartfelt cry to 'awaken love' on earth to and from the people of God. A divine wooing of our hearts will bring us closer to becoming intimate with our Bridegroom King, Jesus.

The cry of 'Yes, Lord' needs to come from our hearts as well as our mouths as we move into the deep waters of our relationship with Him. All our senses need to be awakened and electrified, to come fully alive and be one with Him. This is our inheritance as the people of God, as those who know Him and love Him. One to one, face to face, hearts seeking and finding our beloved Jesus. We seek Your face, Jesus, and we long to be even closer to You. Driven by our desire to see You and to know You more I give You my 'yes' today!

What does it look like for us to give our lives to Him? What does it mean to focus on the Lord without distraction? It takes determination in us to say yes and walk out our faith daily. I believe that if we can say yes, then success can—not *could* but *can*—be measured in our hearts' continued yes to Him. Yielding our will and determination to the way of the Lord and His will is key. Submission to God is the only way we can advance successfully in our faith journey and walk with Him.

Submit yourselves, then, to God... (James 4:7).

Do we have questions, challenges, difficulties and life events to overcome? Absolutely, but we must acknowledge the determination of a heart that says, 'I will not only give You my yes to Your being my Saviour and the Lord of my life, but I will also say yes to anything and everything You have ready for my life. My life is Yours, Jesus! My lifetime and the entire complete time of my life on earth into eternity is Yours—I give it to You now.'

Let us make this our prayer and pulse of our heart, friend, that we might be completely His. Every yes, every agreement with the Lord will take you deeper and closer to Him. Each occasion you set aside with Him, to take time to seek His face and focus your heart on Him, will add to your affirmation of 'I am Yours, Jesus.'

As you journey through your life and relationship with Him, your yes will always be required. Your yielding heart and free will before Him are a sweet fragrance. This is a place of access to Him and His heart. My friend, the more we yield and surrender, the more our love for Him in relation to our submission will take us deeper into intimacy and connection with our Lord and God. 'Seek Me and My face! Come deeper!' Jesus invites us today. The laid-down life is the life alive in Him. Step into the depths of love and give your yes again today.

PRAYER

Lord Jesus, I yield! I give up my own will and my ways in exchange for You, Your will and Your ways. I submit! Take me deeper with You, Lord, now and every day of my life! I long to have a deeper knowledge of You and Your ways both in my heart and being (in accordance with Psalm 86:11). Knowing you Jesus! Knowing you is all I desire. Knowing You in Your death and resurrected life. In Your passion and love of the Father, Your power and light, You who are the Living Word I long to know fully. I count the cost in this moment, yet still I give You my yes, Jesus.

Make this your own prayer. Internalise the words as you say them and connect with what they mean to go deep into your own self. Allow yourself to be moved by the words into a surrendered posture and place of heart—spiritually, emotionally, even physically. He is all! He is worth everything! Jesus is the centre, the heart and the life of all. He desires you to look like Him, to feel like Him, with the full compassionate heart of the Father inside you. His aim is to love you deeply and bring transformation to you completely but it requires your affirmation and agreement. We say yes, Lord Jesus. We say yes! For just as King David said, where else can we go and what else can we do? We must have You, Jesus! (See Psalm 139.)

You may already have laid everything down. 'Thank you', the Lord is saying. If you feel blocked in some way from articulating your yes, I pray for you now. I pray that the Holy Spirit reveals to you in this moment what the issues of your challenge might be. Trust? Fear? Uncertainty? 'Give it to Me', says the Lord. He will move you past the walls that keep you separated from the One who loves you and whom you adore. Step into the place of agreement and choose to say:

> *Lord Jesus, I long to give You my yes—help me move beyond all the issues that are preventing me from completely entering in now. Put a burning in my heart and soul to desire You and You alone, that I may move into the place of being truly one with You. Awaken love for You in me again, Lord Jesus.*

The depths of His love are unfathomable and immeasurable—yet we can enter those depths and experience that fullness of love each time we yield and expose our naked hearts before Him. Give Him your heart, my friend, and you will never regret the yes. You will never be more fully alive or awake!

Your yes is the access to the deeper elements, the greater revelation and the wisdom by the Spirit of God. He is the opening to the deep waters. Without Him all is lost and empty; with Him we are moved by love into the depths of the knowledge of God.

> *These are the things God has revealed to us by his Spirit. The Spirit searches all things, even the deep things of God. For who knows a person's thoughts except their own spirit within them? In the same way, no one knows the thoughts of God except the Spirit of God. What we have received is not the spirit of the world, but the Spirit who is from God, so that we may understand what God has freely given us. This is what we speak, not in words taught us by human wisdom but in words taught by the Spirit, explaining spiritual*

realities with Spirit-taught words (1 Corinthians 2:10-13).

A life-laid down to God opens the door to deep riches of wisdom and revelation. We see this in the life of Samuel the prophet who, before he was conceived, was given to the Lord by his mother and entered the House of God's worship at a young age.

Allow God to draw you in further as you remember Samuel and his experience. Read First Samuel 3 and ask the Lord to speak to you from it. There was a call; the Lord spoke his name. Once. Twice. Three times. 'Samuel!' Understanding came to the young Samuel that it was the Lord, not his master Eli calling him. So Samuel lay down and said aloud, *'Speak, Lord, for Your servant is listening'* (see 1 Samuel 3:9-10 BSB).

In Samuel's heart posture of a servant, alongside the physical position of lying prostrate before the Lord, he released words which opened himself to the Lord and pushed open the door of revelation. The boy's decision initially to respond to Eli and say, 'Here I am!' caused a shift in the heavens to earth. Where vision and revelation were previously rare (1 Samuel 3:1), Samuel's response allowed all the people in the region to hear the word of God and acknowledge Samuel as the prophet; the one whom Scripture says was the only one whose words did not *fall to the ground* but all came to pass because the Lord was with Samuel (1 Samuel 3:19).

There is an invitation to you from the Lord today, to open yourself up to deeper understanding and revelation as Samuel did. Take time to position yourself and to work with the Holy Spirit on any areas of challenge you are facing. When you find yourself finally surrendered on the floor, there will be an immersion in

Him that you have not experienced before. Friend, your life will never be the same and your joy will be made complete. This will bring you to a place of wisdom through intimacy and God will speak in many ways to you from then on.

BAPTISE ME, LORD!

If you have yet to experience the baptism of Holy Spirit, I encourage you to seek the Lord for this amazing and wonderful gift from God. This baptism will transform you. It will bring you into a place of supernatural desire for the Lord, a passionate burning that you cannot work up by yourself. The crashing in of the power of the Spirit on to and into your body will bring a divine exchange that you cannot describe fully to others. Explosive; dynamite power; immersing and flooding your heart, mind and body; empowering you; transforming you in minutes in a supernatural way; these are some of the descriptions that can be your experience.

John the Baptist spoke of it:

> *I baptise you with water for repentance. But after me comes one who is more powerful than I, whose sandals I am not worthy to carry. He will baptise you with the Holy Spirit and fire* (Matthew 3:11).

Jesus prophesied that the Holy Spirit was coming to His followers as He was preparing to leave them:

> *I will ask the Father, and he will give you another helper who will be with you forever. That helper is the Spirit of Truth. The world cannot accept him because it doesn't see or know him. You know him because, he*

lives with you and will be in you (John 14:16-17
GOD'S WORD Translation).

We see the manifestation of Holy Spirit and the baptism of
fire released at Pentecost in Acts 2. Followers of Jesus Christ on
earth were praying and seeking Him together. As the Spirit was
poured out in fire, they were burned alive in the spirit, transformed for all time. They began speaking in other languages—
tongues of men and angels—fully empowered to speak the power
of the Gospel of the Kingdom and to release the Kingdom's
signs, wonders and miracles. They were equipped for the works
of the Kingdom and burned alive, marked forever. Refresh yourself with the Scripture and read Acts 2.

This burning, subsuming baptism is yours in Christ.
Whatever you have struggled with will be given a whole new
perspective through the baptism of Spirit and fire! My friend,
you will come alive in ways you never imagined! This powerful blessing is yours in Christ Jesus. Whether this is your first
time or you are asking for a fresh infilling and immersion, the
following are some words you can use to help you pray and
position yourself.

PRAYER

*Lord Jesus, I ask for the Spirit of Truth, our Advocate
and Helper the Holy Spirit, to come and baptise me.
Completely immerse me in Your Spirit, God! I open
myself—body, soul and spirit—to You now and say
I long to be fully consumed by You. Saturated and
overflowing with who You are, I desire to be burned
with Your fire so that I may be filled with passion*

for You; burn me, Lord, whatever that looks like and whenever You choose.

Over the years I have heard many testimonies of the baptism of Spirit and fire. Not one has been the same as another. Each one is unique, weighty and beautiful. I have prayed for a number of hungry people of all ages and seen the Holy Spirit come and fill them in ways that look different to the naked eye. Some manifest with much weeping, others with the electric power of the Spirit running through their bodies; some are shaking and trembling under the power of God. Many can stand and many are prostrate under the powerful force of God surging through their bodies.

Some are baptised in the process of deliverance from demonic spirits, which scream as they leave—the Spirit of God burns them out along with marking the person being delivered forever. Not one experience is the same as another. I know of people who were with others in prayer at the time; others where the baptism happened to them individually, when they were alone seeking the Lord in privacy. You will have your own testimony.

The testimony of Jesus is the Spirit of prophecy (Revelation 19:10); and so, as I share my own testimony with you, I pray it will open your life to stronger encounters with the Spirit of God in any way He desires to touch you and in the times He has prepared for you.

My personal experience occurred when I was co-leading an Alpha course for the young mothers in our church (of whom I was one). We were sitting in front of the TV having watched the course series video. Our wonderful church minister,

Nigel Barge, prayed for the Holy Spirit to come and fill us. We had heard Nicky Gumbel explain on the video that, for some, it can feel like a pilot light when lit in the boiler; for others it is like a rush of power being released. As Nigel prayed, I felt the power of God flood my body—every part of my insides alive with what I can only describe as a current of spiritual electricity. Water was pouring out of my eyes like rivers and dripping down my neck. My breathing was unusual, and I felt the physical, actual expansion of my heart under the power of God. It was like someone was stretching and pulling my heart into an increased size and capacity. Its rhythm was erratic and random. I felt as if I were going to die! I was praying internally, 'God, I know this is You, but I think You are going to kill me! I want more of You but please stop…no, please I want more!'

Following this power surge, I couldn't use my legs for quite some time after—it was like they didn't belong to me anymore! When I was able to move again, following some recovery time sitting quietly, I joined my friends and heard some of their experiences. All different and distinctive. However, that day in 2007 changed me forever. I had invested in Bible study, every week for five years with my amazing friends. Yet, in that moment the word of God became alive in me in a wholly different way. I felt so alive and so on fire for God! This was the day I remember in great detail because it was the day I was burned and marked forever. Nothing after that was ever the same again.

Two weeks prior to this life-changing event, I had finally succumbed to the nudge I felt inside to go to the front of the church after Sunday service and ask for prayer. I had no idea what I was going to ask for; this was part of the reason I had put it off for a few weeks. But that Sunday I felt pushed to go and ask. I approached the people offering prayers, and when they asked, 'What can we pray for?', I broke down in tears, much to my own surprise and theirs. I replied, 'I have no idea what I am asking for! I just know I want more of God. I want to go to the next level with God but don't know what that looks like!'

Looking back, I believe my desire for more opened me up for what was coming—the baptism. I had no idea then what this looked like or even that I could ask for it. So I want to encourage you, friend, that even if you do not have the words, simply allow your desire for God to increase. Worship Him. Give Him your adoration and focus and God will bring you there Himself. Go with the nudges. If you feel the Lord is leading you in a certain way to receive prayer from another, or you are drawn by the Spirit of God to set yourself a focused time apart to seek Him alone, I encourage you to do just that. The Lord Himself will lead you into your own story of your yes for more.

The Lord says,

'You will seek Me and find Me when you search for Me with all your heart' (Jeremiah 29:13 BSB).

5

Shut Out Darkness

The realm of the spirit opens up to us in a remarkable way. We should celebrate and embrace with joy in Christ alone, for it continually takes us closer to Him and allows us to know Him and His ways more. We can be amazed at what we see and sense but we must not get lost in that separate realm or become separated from Christ.

We must be alert as we enter into this unseen realm. We must acknowledge and hold fast to the strong caution from Scripture always to *'test the spirits'* and know that all spirits who confess Jesus Christ is Lord are from God (1 John 4). We are warned against the prowling lion of the enemy around us (1 Peter 5), to be aware he is an opportunist. Satan disguises himself as an angel of light, so we must exercise our discerning of spirits gift to ensure we are not inadvertently deceived. We do not want to be misled and drawn into the spirit or encounters towards or through anyone other than the Trinity: Father God, Jesus Christ and Holy Spirit.

We want complete clarity and illumination (without any other spiritual interference) by the Spirit of God and no other. We do not partner with fear. We use the wisdom given by God to be alert and ensure we are open only to Him and no one or nothing else. There are some top tips for being aware and dealing with any potential interference from the enemy. These tips will help you avoid some potential pitfalls as you go on this deepening journey of intimacy with the Lord.

Identifying several of the ways in which we may unintentionally be deceived is helpful. The primary recommendations are:

- To be consistent in prioritising due diligence with the Lord Jesus. This will ensure our spiritual access is only to Him and through Him alone.
- To give our lives to Jesus Christ alone and surrender ourselves to His lordship over our lives.
- To repent and be baptised in water—this is the basic premise to closing any other doors that may be open to influence us from our past lives.

Can we have encounters with God before we are saved and have repented? Absolutely we can. Can we see and sense in the spirit before we give our lives to the Lord? Absolutely this is possible because we are fundamentally spirits in a body made in the image of God. God breathed His breath, His Spirit into us when He created us. His ultimate aim is for us to walk with Him in the garden once more, just as Adam did. We are created as spiritual beings.

The question for us must be: is it safe for us to pursue access in the spirit and engage with the spirit realm *without* the blood of Jesus Christ and His name marking us? The short answer is no. My belief is backed up with hearing firsthand experiences from those who became involved in this realm without the Lord and Holy Spirit as their sole guides. I cannot warn you seriously enough against dabbling or attempting to engage in this unseen reality without Jesus Christ. So many lives have been and will be damaged—in some cases ruined—through working with spirits that, like satan, have been thrown out of Heaven.

We know many Christians who are hungry for the supernatural and spiritual encounters but find themselves looking in unhelpful and wrong places. The Word of God is clear: *'Do not turn to mediums or seek out spiritists, for you will be defiled by them. I am the Lord your God'* (Leviticus 19:31).

Spiritualists, mediums and clairvoyants are often working with 'angels' who are disguised demons dressed in a counterfeit light or demonic spirits posing as dead people. Spirit guides and voices from this realm portraying dead people are often familiar spirits that follow families through the generations. They know information which the current living family member believes is real. Necromancy, talking to the dead, is forbidden by God.

Let no one be found among you who...practises divination or sorcery, interprets omens, engages in witchcraft, or casts spells, or who is a medium or spiritist or who consults the dead. Anyone who does these things is detestable to the Lord; because of these same detestable practices the Lord your God will drive out those nations before you. You must be blameless before the Lord your God (Deuteronomy 18:10-13).

The Word of God is explicit. It leaves no room for doubt—seek only God Himself, ask Him alone, not those who speak to the dead.

When someone tells you to consult mediums and spiritists, who whisper and mutter, should not a people inquire of their God? Why consult the dead on behalf of the living? Consult God's instruction and the testimony of warning. If anyone does not speak according to this word, they have no light of dawn (Isaiah 8:19-20).

We see those who operate in divination as well as necromancy can be extraordinarily accurate: in the case in Acts 16 where the slave girl who 'predicted the future' in return for payment. She told all who Paul was and said repeatedly over many days, *'These men are servants of the Most High God, who are telling you the way to be saved.'* Apostle Paul cast out the spirit of divination and she then could no longer 'see the future' (see Acts 16:16-19). The *source* of our revelation is the key. We must only go to God for wisdom and knowledge through Jesus Christ. We must only seek Him, no other. In our search we are invited into the purity and safety of His wisdom and revelation.

Another question needs to be asked: can God reach those who are operating in the spirit this way? I absolutely believe He can and does. The kindness of God leads us to repentance (Romans 2:4) and His ultimate aim is to reconcile all people to Himself. There are numerous testimonies from people who found Jesus Christ from a life of spiritualism or mediumship and encountered Him directly. However, there is an expectation that, once we have given our lives to Jesus Christ, we do not seek information and/or hope from spirits other than the Holy Spirit.

> When I was in Canada on a ministry trip a few years ago, I had an unusual experience. As we were waiting in the hotel lobby to be collected for that day's meetings, a lady I had never met before spoke to me as if she knew me well. 'What are you doing here?', she asked. I was temporarily thrown, but the Holy Spirit informed me that this woman knew me from the realm of the spirit. There had been a medium who had hosted a meeting in the hotel the night before. This lady had been at the meeting and seen me in the spirit realm. I was not aware of this in the natural but as soon as I met her, the Lord revealed this to me.
>
> I politely explained that I was a spirit guide to the living God (using language she understood in the context she had experienced me). I spoke about Jesus Christ being the only way to God and the only way to access the Spirit. She told me she knew God from years ago; she wept as we spoke about Jesus Christ and His love for her. I prophesied over her life and her son. She found the Lord again that morning. Within minutes of our conversation, she had committed her life to Jesus and

promised to go back to church on her return to Nova Scotia.

God will use all means necessary to bring His children back to Him. His ways are mysterious rather than religious. We must be open to God using us in unusual ways and communicating with us supernaturally, with the ultimate goal of finding Him and following Him.

If you have had experience in the spirit realm, accessing a way that was not through Jesus, remember that you are so loved. Come back to Him now. He has made a way for you to be free and at peace, to end the tormenting voices and faces. Speak to the Lord now as you feel able.

Simply cry out to Him saying, *Jesus Christ of Nazareth, I choose You! I give my life to You now. I say You are my Lord and King. Lead me in the way everlasting and reset my spiritual senses. Edit my memory and emotions, Lord, I ask to forget the torment. Close the doors to the spiritual dimensions previously opened as I choose You as my access to the Father and Holy Spirit. Only You, Jesus, and only Your ways. I choose You.'*

CLOSE ALL THE DOORS

Our heart's goal is to follow Jesus Christ alone and not to be deceived. It is absolutely essential that we set clean hands and pure hearts before the Lord in all aspects of our life as much as we are convicted by the Holy Spirit. *'Search me, God, and know my heart!'* (Psalm 139:23) must be the cry of our hearts. We must regularly come before God and ask Him to check that what we are sensing and seeing is not unwittingly through partnership with the demonic. By opening spiritual doors through divination we may inadvertently open ourselves to something that can injure or trap us.

> *Whoever digs a pit may fall into it; whoever breaks through a wall may be bitten by a snake* (Ecclesiastes 10:8).

Knowing God is kind, slow to anger and abounding in love, we come to Him to allow the Holy Spirit to illuminate where we may have erred unintentionally. We do not approach this challenge with fear or trepidation. We come boldly, as people who know who their God is. We know by whom we are empowered. By and through the Holy Spirit and Christ within us, we can make a framework around our spiritual lives in accordance with biblical principles.

We will now look at the individual areas where we could be caught and injured if we do not take the time to do our own spiritual health check, to ensure all unhelpful openings are closed.

Door to Unforgiveness

The door to offence and unforgiveness must be closed. Jesus makes it plain we will not be forgiven by the Father unless we forgive. As we enter into encountering the Lord in increasing measure, we must permanently keep closed the door to unforgiveness. As Paul instructs here, satan will use it to his full advantage otherwise:

> *Anyone you forgive, I also forgive. And what I have forgiven—if there was anything to forgive—I have forgiven in the sight of Christ for your sake, in order*

that Satan might not outwit us. For we are not unaware of his schemes (2 Corinthians 2:10-11).

Maintain a 'closed door policy' to unforgiveness and offence to keep the opportunist out of your life. Allow the Holy Spirit to alert you to anyone or any situation He is inviting you to bring to Him for forgiveness. Take all offence or bitterness to Jesus. He will take it from you. I urge you to take time with Jesus and the Holy Spirit in this area until your heart is released from unforgiveness.

PRAYER AND APPLICATION

Holy Spirit, please shine Your light on my heart and my life and reveal to me any person or situation towards whom I am still holding offence or unforgiveness. I give You access to my life in full and say, Lord, I desire a clean heart in this regard.

Wait on the Lord to hear and sense where or to whom He is directing you. Whatever the situation or the person who is brought to mind, release forgiveness by saying, '*Lord, I choose to forgive. I choose to let go of all offence, releasing them and this situation to You in its fullness.*'

The Lord knows each nuance of the situation you had to go through. Release does not diminish the severity of the impact of the action that caused you pain or grief. In choosing to release forgiveness to God, you are saying to God that you trust Him with the outcome of that issue. If you find yourself struggling to release forgiveness and pardon, pray, '*Lord, my desire is get to the place of being able to forgive this person (name the person). Please help me get there.*'

I encourage you to bring your heart regularly before the Lord and intentionally open it to Him. Keep asking for healing from the pain caused by the person and/or the situation that the Holy Spirit highlighted until you feel able to speak the words, '*Lord, I now forgive NAME and release all my pain, hurt, grief to You.*' It will help to incorporate this into the prayer of seeing and encountering Jesus as seen in Chapter 1. Allow Jesus Himself to minister into any pain this situation and/or memory has caused.

He is not only willing, but Jesus delights in spending time with you and ministering healing to your heart. Simply ask Him to come close and talk to Him as you feel led to do. There is no method, only the relationship and intimacy that He desires with us. I encourage you, friend, to invest yourself in time with Him. You will be overjoyed when you do.

Door to Fear

In our wide experience of training people to sense and see in the spirit, a partnership with fear is the fastest way to put the brakes on any spiritual encounter and operation of our spiritual senses with God. We must deal with any aspect of fear to be free to enter fully into all that is open to us in and through Christ Jesus.

If you recall, I explained in Chapter 2 that fear is one of the loudest spirits in the unseen realm, making a horrible screech that can be heard for miles. We do not want to have a partnership with fear in any form as the demonic can see and hear easily and use it to their advantage. Fear of the demonic, fear of death/sickness, fear of the unknown, fear of the future, of failure... the list goes on. You may have read this Scripture and thought perhaps, 'I hear You, Lord, but I am still afraid!'

For God has not given us a spirit of fear and timidity, but of power, love, and self-discipline (2 Timothy 1:7 NLT).

If you are bound by fear, do not feel condemned; rather, feel convicted to believe there is freedom from it through Christ. I do not know many seers who have not had to 'face off' the demonic in this regard in order to win the victory. Fear loves to intimidate and will try to shut down the gift. The spirits know that if they are sensed and/or seen, we can have the victory over them. In my own case, as God opened more of the spirit realm to me and increased the impact and profound nature of the encounters, it was as if the spirit of fear hunted me down!

ENCOUNTERING THE SPIRIT OF FEAR

The greatest fear I had to overcome was fear of my baby dying. This fear was horrendous and crippling. It was as if the enemy intentionally wanted to shut me down and stop me engaging in the spirit realm. I successfully battled and overcame this fear. If we can engage in the spirit, we can advance the Kingdom of God more effectively and we are a threat to the enemy's influence.

> One night I got up to go to the bathroom, as I did most nights. This time, however, in the darkness, a foreboding and dread fell upon me. I became, in the moment of taking three steps from our bed, a fearful wreck. I was frozen in my tracks. Terror of the dark literally overwhelmed me and I thought, *How am I going to get to the bathroom and back?*
>
> I am a confident person, and I would say that previously I had rarely experienced fear in my life—I

can even parachute out of a plane peacefully and joyfully! This feeling, however, was like a blazing 100W light bulb of fear that was violently switched on. I had no control over it, and it was absolutely horrific!

I can remember creeping my stiff frozen body to the loo and then running back to bed as fast as possible, throwing myself under the covers, my heart racing. After eventually getting back to sleep, I woke up the following morning and convinced myself that it was surely just a one-time occurrence because it was so out of character. However, the following night, I woke from a deep sleep, got up and again, I was completely freaked out—my pulse racing as I felt surrounded by the dark. The thick blackness of fear enveloped me. I stood there for what seemed ages, frozen to the spot. Thank the Lord, my husband, Alastair, woke up and asked what I was doing. I explained and, as I spoke the words 'sudden fear of the dark', I immediately saw an ugly demon in the corner of the room, hiding in the shadows. I went into warrior mode and prayed in the spirit to send it packing! My husband broke the spirit off me after I had repented for partnering with it and it left as fast as it had come! Praise Jesus! And thank God for speedy learns!

Let me reassure you: if you are suffering from any form of fear, it can be as easy for you as it was for me to shift it away. Agreement from us gives the demonic room in our lives. We grant it permission to have that hold on us. Once we identify and expose it, once we break agreement with it intentionally and apply our will not to partner with it, we can be completely free and liberated! Hallelujah!

You may think to yourself, *maybe I can get away with not dealing with this fear I have.* May I ask, my friend, why would you wish to carry an unnecessary weight, to labour under a spirit of fear that is stealing so much joy and fullness of life from you? You will not be able to engage fully in all the Lord has for you, all that is so rich and incredible. If you need further impetus, ask the Holy Spirit to show you what the spirit of fear has stolen from you over the years. You will be shocked and surprised at how much influence it will have had.

PRAYER FOR FREEDOM FROM FEAR

Apply your will and believe with your heart. Desire to expose the spirit and break the power of it over and in your life. I encourage you to come to Jesus and look for and sense Him in the spirit, close to you as you pray. Again, you can go back to the Activation in Chapter 1 to remind yourself. As Jesus is close, pray as the Holy Spirit leads you in that moment and as you hand over your fears to Him. Ask the Lord what He wants to tell you or give you in return.

The following prayer may give you an outline of how you might pray:

> *Father, in the name of Jesus Christ I repent for my partnership with the spirit of fear in all its forms: the ones that I know and the ones that I don't know. Lord, I particularly repent for having partnership*

*with the fear of (NAME IT HERE) and ask for
Your forgiveness. I choose now to break complete
agreement with the spirit of fear in all its forms, and
I tell it to leave me now! I give You all my fears and
receive Your forgiveness and freedom. I step into my
liberation in You, Jesus! I say, I trust You, Lord, and
put all my trust in You for all of my life.*

I encourage you to ask the Holy Spirit to lead your prayers as you partner with the Lord in a life without fear. See what that looks like as He leads you. Invite the Holy Spirit to fill you afresh and overflow in and through you. Ask the Lord for some Scriptures and insights of what your life without fear will look like. Ask the Lord to keep you from fear during the journey.

If you have a spouse or friend who can support you, just as my husband did, that's very helpful. If not, still pray and trust that the Lord will deliver you from the evil of fear. Work with Him. You may gain instantaneous freedom, which I pray you do. However, if fear has been dominant in your life for some time, you may need to hold that ground, day by day, until you are walking in the fullness of that freedom.

DOORS IN THE HOME ENVIRONMENT

We may inadvertently open doors to spirits in our homes and/or property without realising it. This will affect the purity of our spiritual atmosphere and could affect our encounters with the Lord. It is a simple fix. Ask the Holy Spirit to shine His light on your property and land. This will enable you to work with Him in consecrating it to the living God in Jesus' name and in setting a spiritual boundary around what is yours.

Building altars to the Lord and dedicating geographical locations is seen throughout Scripture, as well as tearing down altars and 'poles' built to other gods in the process. We, of course, build our own altars in the spirit through prayer and worship. Locating physical altars to the living God on our properties may not be common today; however, acknowledging your land, home and buildings are the Lord's and no others' is important, especially if there have been other spiritual influences, altars and/or defilements historically. We will often only know this through revelation, which is why I suggest you seek the Lord as you pray both for and in your home and property.

The earth is the Lord's, and everything in it, the world, and all who live in it (Psalm 24:1).

Years ago, before I really knew Jesus Christ personally or had had any spiritual encounters, we experienced a 'spirit' in our home, which was not the Holy Spirit. Following the birth of our son, we had employed a part-time nanny to take care of him while I was at work. After a few months' working with us, she told us that she was upset and disturbed by some odd occurrences. She kept hearing music going on and off downstairs when she was upstairs; when she went downstairs, it stopped. Furthermore, the light in the utility room kept randomly going on and off. She explained that she had an uneasy feeling with these 'signs' and, simultaneously, she felt that something or someone was present.

We had no experience with anything like this before. We were attending church at this time but hadn't committed our lives to the Lord. Then I too noticed the light issue, but I never heard the music. This only occurred when she was alone in the house.

Soon after, we were at a family lunch when I, half-jokingly, said to our local church minister, 'I think we might have a ghost!' I explained the odd occurrences. He became very quiet and serious looking, which threw me! He reassured me that he believed me; he believed he had experienced the supernatural nature of God of light, and the supernatural nature of the devil and his darkness. There had been occasions when he had prayed 'cleansing prayers' in homes in our village. I was intrigued. I was certainly never distressed by this which I believe was a gift from God.

Our minister offered to come and give prayers of cleansing or, he suggested, we could do it ourselves. Armed with his suggested prayer, I stood in our utility room and spoke to the flickering light, 'This house is for Jesus Christ and no other, the Holy Spirit and no other! All other spirits must leave now!' Literally from the moment this prayer of declaration left my mouth, we had no other issues.

We found out later that our nanny had been to a psychic for an annual 'spiritual reading'. The time she had had this reading was about the same time she had begun to experience the strange happenings in our home. As the owner of the house, I closed the door she had inadvertently opened—job done!

Thus began a journey of understanding for me—what we partner with spiritually has a cause and effect in our lives and homes. Over time, having been trained with the Holy Spirit to review everything, I understood that what was on our bookshelves, in our DVD library (yes I am that old!), what hung on our walls, our mementoes and ornaments, all could be portals (open doors). I realised that spiritual influences exist in what can seem the most innocuous objects. However, the approach is simple. With the Holy Spirit, review your home and your property and do what He tells you; pray and follow His lead.

This spiritual review is best done taking each room one at a time. Try to sense with the Holy Spirit what, if anything, feels 'off' spiritually and then discern why. Some things may have been passed down through inheritance and carry attachments to the dead person. A simple cleansing prayer over the item, anointing with oil in Jesus' name, breaking off in the spirit anything that belongs to them should deal with the issue. Other items may be more obviously dark: anything associated with horror; the sexually explicit; witchcraft; demonically inspired objects including music, books, images or films. When you review and work through, room by room, with the Holy Spirit, you will sense with ease what can be anointed and kept—and what needs to be disposed of.

More extreme variations could be New Age or occult and/ or witchcraft books and items in various forms; freemasonry clothing/jewellery/bibles (the name of Jesus is omitted); false gods, such as buddha, or other images or icons of false gods. These create a spiritual atmosphere and could have potentially opened spiritual doors of influence that you will need to shut as the Holy Spirit directs you.

When your review is complete and the space is dedicated to the living God in Jesus' name, the atmosphere in your home, room, workspace, etc. will feel spiritually cleaner and clearer. In a shared space it is simple to dedicate your room, your desk and seat area to the living God and 'set it apart'. If you own the home, building and/or land, I encourage you to dedicate all that is yours to God. We see this modelled in Scripture, in the great prophets such as Abraham and Jacob who built altars to the Lord everywhere they camped. We can take anointing oil and pour it on the land, delineating it in the name of Jesus Christ and setting our homes and property apart for His glory alone. We can mark our doorposts as the people of God did with the blood of the Lamb at Passover and pray, 'Nothing but the Kingdom of God and for His glory!'

LEARNING SPIRITUAL ATMOSPHERE LESSONS

On a family holiday in Sardinia, we came across a wonderful looking antiquarian shop which intrigued us from the outside. I began climbing up the steps to the shop, intending to follow my family inside. I got two steps from the door and was literally, physically thrown back in the spirit by an invisible force. An instant holy shout started to form in my belly at the force of the oppressive demonic atmosphere. On further inspection

I saw one side of the shop was filled with statues and images of various gods. It was the force of the dark spiritual atmosphere that threw me back. Be aware.

If you love collecting figures of idols and/or gods, you are unwittingly creating an altar to them in your home, garden or workplace. You are creating an unclean spiritual atmosphere through them which could open a door you would not wish to be opened. These images cannot remain. You may not be intentionally worshipping them, but just by giving them a home, you are giving the spirits associated with them potential access to your house and the opportunity to pollute your atmosphere spiritually. Our God is a jealous God, and He will not give glory to another, and we must not either.

First Samuel 5 illustrates this unseen force of the power of God against the unseen force of a demonic god:

> *When the Philistines took the ark of God, they brought it into the house of Dagon and set it by Dagon. And when the people of Ashdod arose early in the morning, there was Dagon, fallen on its face to the earth before the ark of the Lord. So they took Dagon and set it in its place again. And when they arose early the next morning, there was Dagon, fallen on its face to the ground before the ark of the Lord. The head of Dagon and both the palms of its hands were broken off on the threshold; only Dagon's torso was left of it. Therefore neither the priests of Dagon nor any who come into Dagon's house tread on the threshold of Dagon in Ashdod to this day (1 Samuel 5:2-5 NKJV).*

As we exalt God in our homes and workplaces, other gods must bow the knee and be on their faces before Him. We shift and change the spiritual atmosphere in our homes by worshipping the one true God and displacing any other influence.

ACTIVATION AND PRAYER

The following is a suggested outline of how to respond in your own spaces. There is no method to this, but by simply following the lead of the Spirit of God you will enable your home to be a dwelling for only the Holy Spirit.

Take time with the Holy Spirit to pray and ask Him to alert you to anything that may be interfering with your spiritual atmosphere or creating a potential access point for demonic spirits. I encourage you not to go digging in your memory, just sit with the Lord and ask Him, by the Spirit of God, to bring anything to mind. Walk round each room asking the Holy Spirit to open your spiritual senses to anything that may be problematic, then ask the Lord what He recommends you do with it.

Some items could be triggers to emotional pain and, for that reason, the Lord will convict you that it is time for those items to be removed from your home, workplace, business etc, so you can receive the fullness of your healing. Remove and dispose of each as you feel led.

I encourage you, friend, to anoint your home and property to God and to 'build an altar of worship' to Him in your house and business. It is as simple as taking some oil—olive or any anointing oil—and using it in the way you feel the Holy Spirit is leading you. For example, mark your external doors, gates, entrance ways and windows with oil. You may feel led to plant something or place stones as a prophetic act. Go where the Holy Spirit leads you. As you do, pray a dedication to the Most High God in Jesus' name alone and decree:

> *Nothing may enter this place other than from the Kingdom of God. Holy Spirit be the only Spirit in this home! We welcome You, Holy Spirit, to invade and fill this place. I set it apart for Your fruitfulness and glory. Lord God, in the name of Jesus Christ, I dedicate our/my home to You. What I have is Yours and I say is this is Your space and place. I am Yours. I ask that You reveal everything in my home, workplace, business that may be affecting the spiritual atmosphere. I ask for all that is contrary to Your Kingdom to be seen and that You convict me of anything that may be affecting me and/or my family, co-workers etc. unknowingly.*

Once this spiritual review is complete you will experience such a positive shift in your atmosphere. I prophesy you will encounter the Lord in increasing measure and access the realm of the spirit with ease. You will have dreams, visions and supernatural experiences like never before with the living God.

GENERATIONAL 'OCCULT' (HIDDEN) DOORS

Another area to focus on, where we may have inadvertently put a hole in our own hedge, is through unknown generational curses (God made a hedge around Job as protection; see Job 1:10). The Word of God is clear that we are all responsible for our own sin. We are not responsible for our forebears' sin, but we could be labouring under a bloodline curse which they knowingly, or in most cases unknowingly, initiated.

We are again using our spiritual senses that are being awakened to seek the Lord about something that may affect our own and/or our family's lives. We cannot do this by information alone. We may know our forebears were freemasons, for example, who do not worship through Jesus Christ but, as one discovers, through the 33 degrees vows and belief structure based on luciferianism (lucifer the angel of light whom we know as satan). Perhaps they were active in witchcraft or New Age worship; perhaps they sought help or influence from these spiritual influences in their lives.

> *You shall not bow down to them or worship them; for I, the Lord your God, am a jealous God, punishing the children for the sin of the parents to the third and fourth generation of those who hate me* (Deuteronomy 5:9).
>
> *And he passed in front of Moses, proclaiming, 'The Lord, the Lord, the compassionate and gracious God, slow to anger, abounding in love and faithfulness, maintaining love to thousands, and forgiving wickedness, rebellion and sin. Yet he does not leave the guilty unpunished; he punishes the children and their children for the sin of the parents to the third and fourth generation'* (Exodus 34:6-7).

Three or four generations could be up to 100 years prior to our being alive. Potentially, if our unknown forebears rejected God or worshipped other gods, we may be labouring under this curse. The opposite is true if we worship God and follow His ways. We are blessed and God deals with those who curse us.

*I will bless those who bless you, and whoever curses
you I will curse; and all peoples on earth will be blessed
through you* (Genesis 12:3).

*but showing love to a thousand generations of those who
love me and keep my commandments* (Exodus 20:6).

We will never know all the things our forebears partnered
with spiritually just by our own knowledge or family information. We need to rely on the Holy Spirit to guide us and illuminate anywhere there is a door open or potential hole in our
hedge that needs sealing.

In the case of generational curses, they may often be activated when we ourselves have been involved in false god worship
or partnered with other gods in seemingly innocent actions.
For example, we may have been curious about the occult, tried
using a Ouija board, had a tarot-card reading, attended a séance,
visited a spiritualist church and more. These may not have had
a massive influence at the time but, as we give our lives to Jesus
Christ and come under His stewardship, these issues can became
a more obvious obstruction. They can impact the grace of our
relationship with Him if we have not specifically repented and
been delivered from any demonic spirits associated with them.
It is then we need to seek the Lord. This is when we must pray
Psalm 139:23-24 (NKJV) as David prayed, *'Search me, O God,
and know my heart; try me, and know my anxieties; and see if there
is any wicked way in me and lead me in the way everlasting.'*

God will reveal these areas of potential generational influences to you. They are easily yet soberly dealt with through
repentance and seeking forgiveness from the Lord for these
acts of intentional or unintentional worship of other gods. We

have ministered to many people over the years; people who have innocently done something as simple as visited a foreign god's temple as a tourist. Even the act of taking off their shoes as requested by the tour guide may have significantly affected them and allowed the spirits worshipped at that temple to open a generational door to false god worship. As they stepped in, this curse was activated. Hundreds of Christians have received freedom from ancestral involvement in occult practices and freemasonry. The Lord has shone His light and the sin of the forebears was appropriated to the cross of Jesus, thus bringing complete freedom. These curses are not difficult for the Lord to remove.

> In one of our multiple Freedom Days from freemasonry at GPA, we had an amazing young man (we shall call him N) who had been tormented by spirits of rage and anger. He could not find peace no matter what he tried. N was easily triggered into a blinding rage to the point of wanting to attack people. Even though he loved Jesus and had given his life to Him, his training as a boxer had allowed these spirits to gain powerful influence and access. This was due to previous family generational worship through the freemasonry structure. As N was led in his complete submission to God to renounce the vows made by his ancestors, he was able to attain complete freedom. N proclaimed that he had never felt the love of God like he did in that moment of freedom. It was beautiful to watch this angry demon of rage being forced to release its hold over this delightful young man;

to see him come into such a sense of joy and peace as he had never experienced previously. Our God is amazing at bestowing liberation and freedom when we submit to Him!

Regarding freemasonry, we have met people who could not get a breakthrough in financial matters and then receive massive pay increases or inheritances within days or weeks of gaining freedom in Christ. Those who couldn't get pregnant for years were with child within short periods of time; those with specific illnesses were cured and enjoyed complete freedom and healing in all areas through repentance and renouncement of all vows in the 33 degrees. Praise God, I, along with many others, was healed years ago of the asthma that nearly killed me as a child due to the generational curse associated with freemasonry (asthma is quite a common illness within freemasonry).

As we practise using our spiritual senses, the Holy Spirit will convict us of any generational curses *if* there are any and reveal their root as we pray for revelation. The more we press into God and go deeper with Him, the more these hindrances can be revealed. The Lord, in His kindness, will lead us to repentance. He will give us the opportunity to be free of all with the ultimate aim of going deeper with God and knowing Him more.

PRAYER FOR REVELATION

Remember, it is through the confession of our mouths that we are free. Prayers like these are always best spoken out loud and not internalised.

Holy Spirit, I ask that You reveal to me any generational curses and doors that may have been opened in my family line, that I may bring them to You, God, for repentance and complete freedom from all curses. Spirit of wisdom and revelation, please open my eyes. Lord, I long to have a deep connection with You and desire all hindrances to be removed from me. Here I am, Your servant. I am listening and watching.

Expect revelation to come in various forms including reading the Word of God, visions, encounters and dreams. Pay attention to what the Lord is revealing and press into that until complete freedom is won. Sometimes it is a journey of healing and process, at other times there is immediate freedom. The more yielded to God we are, the easier this process is. Expect the revelation to come and be alert to the Lord. Be intentional in watching and listening—not in concern but with the knowledge of the reality of Christ in you and the hope of glory that will bring you into the fullness of liberation.

Submit yourselves, then, to God. Resist the devil, and he will flee from you (James 4:7).

As the Lord reveals to you any generational issues, pray He leads you to specific repentance for what He has revealed. As you say the words, apply your will to break agreement with all hindrances associated with any generational curses.

PRAYER FOR REPENTANCE

Lord, in the name of Jesus Christ I repent for all of my own and my ancestors' partnership with (false god worship, witchcraft, freemasonry or whatever the Holy Spirit has revealed to you) and ask for Your forgiveness on my and their behalf. I choose now to break agreement with all partnership with these spirits (name them) and say I belong to You and You alone, Lord Jesus. I completely submit to You and Your ways. I ask that You expose and relieve me now of every spirit associated with this ancestral issue. I ask, Lord, that all associated family curses are now broken from me and my family line and receive my freedom.

DOOR TO WITCHCRAFT

If you, or others in your family, encounter interference in visions and experiences with the Lord or if you are seeing more dark and demonically inspired things rather than the light, the Kingdom of God and heavenly inspired visions or dreams from the Lord, this may reveal the door that was opened to witchcraft in your family history. If you personally have been involved in any form of witchcraft before you found Jesus Christ, as you pursue God further you may find a tension and challenge in trying to go deeper with the Lord and that intimacy is elusive. Ask the Holy Spirit to reveal this to you and for the root of the issue to be revealed.

Witchcraft books, tarot cards and similar objects are increasingly more available in mainstream stores, bookstores and on the Internet. What was once historically exclusive and had to be intentionally sought, has now become extremely easy to access. There seems to be a cultural trend and focus, particularly with teenagers, for media on occult issues to be readily available— there are even workshops on basic witchcraft spells in many places. New Age practices and other religious ceremonies have become blended with modern culture. They are seen as harmless but we must be aware, my friend, that dabbling in any form of occult practice is potentially very harmful—with or without Jesus in your life—and should be a definite closed door for those who follow Jesus Christ. Any experience in this area will pollute a person's relationship with the Lord and can lead to great difficulty. Please stay away from any form of occult practice, even out of curiosity. You will be grateful you did.

I can tell you many life stories of people who have been deceived by the enemy regarding this subject. They have been knocked off track completely. While they see and sense things in the spirit, these things are not of God; but people believe all the while that they are, thus losing themselves and their faith in the process. We know of people who have been hurt physically, emotionally and mentally through dabbling as well as getting involved with generational witchcraft or mediumship. Please be warned and stay well clear. It can all seem safe until you try to free yourself; then people realise the major spiritual battle it can be.

Witches and those operating in the occult use something called the 'third eye' to see in the spirit. This point sits between the eyebrows on the forehead. It could be that you are still seeing through the open 'third eye' if your family or you personally operated in this spiritual realm. You may have confused or unpleasant visions and spiritual experiences until it is dealt with. The 'eye' needs to be closed to allow you to be free to move with the Lord in the spirit.

Following repentance as before, my suggestion is to pray while anointing your forehead with oil. Pray the following and shut it off completely.

PRAYER

Father God, in the name of Jesus Christ, I repent for every way I or those in my family line partnered with all forms of witchcraft and worked in or accessed the spirit realm through the use of the third eye. (With your anointed hand on the centre of your forehead say) I now choose to close the third eye completely in the name of the Father, Son and Holy Spirit, decreeing that it is sealed shut by the blood and name of Jesus Christ of Nazareth. I ask that You edit my memory and emotions from seeing and sensing all things seen through this eye.

It is crucial to destroy any books or items associated with the form of witchcraft you or your family were associated with—we see this principle in Acts 19:19:

A number who had practised sorcery brought their scrolls together and burned them publicly. When they calculated the value of the scrolls, the total came to fifty thousand drachmas.

There is a huge harvest of souls coming from those who have been deceived in the darkness of occult practices—from the 'lite' end of New Age to the dark black of witchcraft and satanism. We need to understand that the gift of seeing and sensing in the spirit enables us, as born-again ones, to partner more effectively with the Holy Spirit. In this way, we can help these souls to become completely liberated as they yield their lives to the lordship of Jesus Christ.

Revelation, words of knowledge and wisdom will come to you to help set them free and you will see the Lord at work in their lives through the Spirit of God. It is an incredible privilege to co-labour with God.

There is also a mass harvest coming from those who believed they were Christian churchgoers but went looking for spiritual encounters and experiences in the wrong places, such as spiritual fairs, spiritualist churches, clairvoyants or mediums. We have met many people hungry for God and for encounters with Him. However, they were unintentionally accessing spiritual 'revelation' through demonic methods and causing themselves all manner of difficult challenges and issues.

We need to be those who ask for wisdom and revelation for ourselves from the true God and for His truth for the sake of those we love. We need to warn people about the dangers of the occult by stepping into the fullness of life and helping others to do the same.

6

UNDER AUTHORITY

A shooting, burning pain went through my collarbone. I was in agony and, through my tears, I cried out to the Lord, 'What are You doing, Jesus?'

I was attending a healing conference as a delegate. One evening and then again the following morning during worship, I had felt hands touch my shoulders, one each side. On each occasion I turned round but I saw no one touching me. However, both times just before I felt the pressure of the touch, I saw a vision of two hands, palms up, before me. There were holes in both palms and I knew at once they were Jesus' hands touching me. This was incredible in itself. The surge of the presence of God all over my body was glorious… until the burning sensation and penetrating pain increased on and in my collarbone. I put up my hand to touch the bone and it then became absolute agony!

Everyone around me was lost in worship, and I was crying in pain but also weeping under the presence of God. I was a hot mess saying, 'Jesus, what are You doing to me?', over and over. I began to rub at the intense pain on my left side. Then I realised that something remarkable was happening. I could feel the egg-shaped deformity on my collarbone starting to straighten out under my hand as I touched it. The bump flattened as the heat and pain came in concentrated waves. After a time, I realised I had been completely healed and the collarbone was restored to its original perfect shape. I was 35 years old when this miracle happened.

When I was 11 years old, I had an accident at school and broke my left arm and collarbone. Unhelpfully, my collarbones fused back together leaving me with a bony, egg-shaped bump and restricted movement in my shoulder. When I lay down on my back for example, my left shoulder did not touch the floor. I had had considerable discomfort through my early teens and beyond, which was not helped with excruciating cortisone injections from giant-sized needles! After years of discomfort, I had become used to pain on a damp day, but the accident itself was a dim memory.

Until Jesus remembered. He came to touch me that May day and completely straightened out the bone—supernatural alignment and healing without anyone else praying for me or by me asking God for healing. Sovereignly, Jesus chose to touch me and brought my shoulders into line by releasing the bone. He knows absolutely every detail of our bodies and lives.

As you might imagine, this encounter led me to pursue more of God and His supernatural ways. I never dreamt anything so amazing and incredible could happen to anyone, least of all to me. This miraculous intervention was astonishing in itself. However, with hindsight I can see the greater significance. Jesus was preparing me to be ready to carry the weight of His authority which is for us all in Christ.

WHO HAS AUTHORITY?

Then Jesus came to them and said, 'All authority in heaven and on earth has been given to me. Therefore go...' (Matthew 28:18-19).

There is never any question if Jesus' authority is limited. His governmental remit for Heaven and earth is secure and certain for all time. He proclaims *all* authority is His! At His name, every knee must bow and every tongue confess that He is Lord (Philippians 2:10-11). Because Jesus Christ, our God who is Three in One, has all authority no other god, spirit, power or principality has any. None. No other. Only Jesus.

Jesus announces His authority and then commands us, His disciples, to go in and under that authority that is His alone. We go as anointed ones—those who go 'in Christ'. As our King and Lord, our Commander in Chief, we go with the same authority when we speak in His name or do something He has directed us to by His Word or Spirit. We then move and operate as if it were Jesus Himself speaking. Christ in us, the hope of glory! Alive in Christ! We are in Him and He in us. We are one with Him.

We all have all authority in Christ—there is never a moment, once you have given your life to the lordship of King Jesus, that you do not have it. As Christians we are often not aware of it or we believe in some way that it is diminished or limited. Jesus said *all* authority was His and yet He only did what He saw the Father do (see John 5:19). He did not move out on His own or in His own understanding or knowledge. He watched the Father closely and acted as He did—He spoke into what the Father was saying and doing.

We must be ones who understand that to be people of authority we must come under that authority. If we are speaking in Jesus' name, we must be assured we are speaking what Jesus is saying and doing at that point in time, if it is in line with His word to us. That is why having our senses alive and awake to the spirit realm is so crucial, my friend! It allows us to partner closely with what the Lord is doing so we can daily move both under and with His authority.

If we consider the centurion who came to see Jesus in Matthew 8, he was moved with such great compassion for his servant that he requested Jesus to heal him. This man completely comprehended the extent of the authority Jesus walked under. He saw that if Jesus spoke the word of healing, then his servant instantly would be supernaturally healed. He understood, due to his military perspective on authority, that Jesus did not need to be within physical proximity to his servant to achieve the miracle:

…just say the word, and my servant will be healed… (Matthew 8:8).

Jesus was amazed at the centurion's response and declared His astonishment at this soldier's incredible faith in and understanding of Jesus' authority. This is such an important lesson for us to grasp. The military mindset of the soldier is complete obedience—when faced with a superior who says, 'Go', he goes. 'Advance', he advances. 'Stand down', he stands down. The soldier is repeatedly drilled in the basic principles of obedience to those commands from authority. He is trained to do *what* he is told to do *when* he is told to do it. We can learn much from the soldier's understanding, my friend. When the Lord says to us, 'Move', we move; 'Rest', we rest; 'Go', we go. Our obedience is key for operating under the Lord's authority. We know how much God values obedience—it is *'better than sacrifice'* (1 Samuel 15:22). Let us learn obedience to move under the authority of Jesus Christ.

PRAYER OF RESPONSE

Lord, I choose right now to say I come under Your authority! I am willing to go where and when You say go. I am willing to move as You lead, Lord—to see and sense what You are doing and move with You. From today I choose to be obedient to You.

Once we learn to be the ones who submit to God's authority and respond when He asks us, we will find He directs us and moves in and through us in greater measure. As we become ones who are trusted to obey every time, we are increasingly given instruction and are released to operate in the authority we have come under.

The Spirit of the Lord will instruct you and lead you to act and speak, with the full weight of His authority, as if He Himself were speaking, because you have submitted completely. Much like in the army, there can be expansion in influence and promotion as we prove ourselves diligent to the word of the Lord. Our remit can grow in influence; it can be expanded if we are conscientious with all the Lord has given us to fulfil day by day.

THE KEY TO AUTHORITY IS ON YOUR SHOULDERS

It is accepted military practice worldwide to represent a soldier's rank and authority with epaulettes. So too, the Lord draws attention to shoulders to mark His authority and government. Just as Jesus Christ wears His authority of God's government on His shoulders—as proclaimed in Isaiah 9:6 '...*the government will be on his shoulders*'—the Lord now touches your shoulders today and reminds you of the weight of authority He desires to put on yours.

Take a moment to acknowledge the Lord touching you and placing the weight of His hands on you today. He is calling you to carry the Lord's burden of His rule and governance. This burden and weight is unique to you, bespoke to your calling in Christ. It is a privilege. The weight of God's rule is a light burden for those who are called.

> *I will place on his shoulder the key to the house of David; what he opens no one can shut, and what he shuts no one can open* (Isaiah 22:22).

We operate in the authority of Christ. The authority that has been given to those who are in Him and have submitted to His lordship with speech and action will enable you to enter the place where Isaiah 22:22 becomes a reality. God says open what is before you in the spirit as you are discerning with your senses. He says release the fetters and limitations from an individual or region. When we pray in accordance with His instructions, it will be so. When the Lord says, 'Bind that demon' or 'Shut those gates/doors', as He orders and we speak it, it shall be done on earth as it is in Heaven, just as Jesus said.

> *Truly I tell you, whatever you bind on earth will be bound in heaven, and whatever you loose on earth will be loosed in heaven* (Matthew 18:18).

When God speaks and we react like an obedient soldier, we will see things and experience things we never imagined. Friend, you will see the Lord move and open things you never dreamed. Enjoy this training and lifestyle in submission and obedience to the Lord for it will liberate you and so many others! This key to God's authority, which opens and shuts, loosens and binds in the spirit, is crucial to the 'violent' advancement of the Kingdom of God and His people (see Matthew 11:12). Like Jesus says, *'But if I drive out demons by the finger of God, then the kingdom of God has come upon you* [those we minister to]' (Luke 11:20).

As we are diligent in our submission to the Lord, being the ones trusted with His governmental weight on our shoulders at the time He has set, we will see transformation in individual lives, in our neighbourhoods, towns and cities, our workplaces and our families. We will experience the unseen realm breaking into the natural, earthly realm and see the fruit of our obedience time and again.

Submission Is Key

In my own early years' training with the Lord, I was instructed by Him to go to many geographical locations to pray and discern in the Spirit. He has taken me through what I have come to know as 'spiritual exercises', to learn to discern the spirits and navigate the unseen realm. Often these specific instructions would come when I was on holiday with my family, especially in the Hebrides (a group of islands in Scotland). I would spend my time with the Lord each morning and, on occasion, He would impress upon me or actually speak directly to me, to go to a certain place on the island to wait on Him there. Standing and watching, sensing in the spirit, He would speak to me about why I was there and for what I was to pray. Sometimes this happened with friends when on spiritual retreat together and other times when I was alone in my training phase. On so many occasions over the years God would open my eyes and senses to what was happening in the spirit and I would be completely blown away.

In the beginning of my intense training phase during corporate worship, the Lord would give me instruction to kneel down, stand up, lie down, or go and stand in such a place in the room where I was worshipping. I used to get a little frustrated with these orders as all I longed to do was worship freely; but I responded in obedience as I knew I was being prepared for reacting in an instant. This experience is available to you as the Lord increasingly instructs you.

On one particular occasion, the Lord impressed on me to go to a specific ancient chapel ruin near to where we were staying. As I approached the old ruin I was quietly praying in tongues and keeping myself alert in the spirit. I asked the Lord, 'What do You want me to see and where do You want me to stand?' I had learned by this point that when God told me to position myself in a particular location, the unseen spirit realm would open up to my senses. Then I would encounter the specific things He wanted to reveal to me.

Navigating a herd of cows in the field, with my senses alert from Holy Spirit's leading, I stood inside the ruin, close to an opening that would have been the original doorway. This particular chapel ruin was sixth century and there was little left of the structure. As I stood there, the Lord revealed an open door in the spirit, just beneath my feet. It looked like steps, down from where I was standing, into the depths below. I asked the Lord, as we see the prophets in Scripture ask, 'What is this, Lord?' I was told it was an ancient demonic entrance and I was to close it. I had no idea how to do that and so I asked the sensible question, 'How shall I do this, Lord?' I was then instructed to sit down on it and say simply, 'I close this door in Jesus' name.' I did as instructed.

While watching and looking in the spirit, I saw and heard a door slam shut. Amazed at the ease of the words coming out of my mouth and the action that followed in the spirit, I sat for a time contemplating this. I was then told to say, 'I seal this shut in the name of the Father, Son and Holy Spirit. Be sealed.' As I spoke the words aloud, the door disappeared completely from view.

The Lord said, 'Stand up!' I stood up, continuing to watch and look in the spirit. My senses were attentive as the Lord said to me, 'Do you see that door before you?' As I looked, a large door directly in front of me appeared. It was perhaps eight feet in height, slightly raised off the ground and situated on the other side of the ancient chapel's doorway. I heard the Lord say, 'Now open this door.'

The door looked almost holographic to me—while I could see the outline in the spirit, I could still see the view of the field, the cows and chapel in the natural. My eyes were open throughout as before. Explaining this was a heavenly door, the Lord gave me the words to say. As I prayed the words out loud, the door flew open and a gust of air came through which I felt in the natural. Almost immediately a rushing sound increased in volume as angels flew out of the door, travelling at intense speed, one after the other, filling the space around the door, the chapel and me! I could feel and hear the swish and rustling of their wings as they exited...tens and tens more came out and filled the field.

I was in awe and shocked! This was the first time I had seen so many angels together and my first spiritual door experience. I heard a term which the Lord has used with me many times since then, 'Mission accomplished.'

We know from Scripture that there are spiritual doors that open. In Revelation 4, John the revelator experienced a door standing open in Heaven. We know that Jacob found himself at Bethel, lying at the bottom of a heavenly opening containing a ladder, and saw angels ascending and descending there. These doors or portals, openings in the spirit, are access points in the natural to the spiritual world on earth. God will reveal openings, both demonic and heavenly, that need to be closed and opened in various contexts. Where there has been partnership with a form of witchcraft for example, there can be demonic openings which God will reveal at the due time of their closing. He will also lead us to open doors at His instruction at their due time.

The follow-up to this amazing encounter and lesson with the Lord came to pass a few months later.

On returning to the island sometime after opening this heavenly door, the Lord encouraged me to watch in the spirit from the upper deck of the ferry that I was travelling on with some friends. We were coming to spend time in retreat with each other and the Lord for a few days. As I looked in the spirit towards the coastline, there were literally hundreds of angels on the land, jumping up and down in excitement at our impending arrival, like a welcome committee! I asked the Lord, 'What is this?' The entire horizon was filled. God explained to me that these were the angels that had come through the door He had asked me to open previously. I was completely blown away.

Walking with God in obedience and surrendering, with our yes in our hearts, ensures that God will always speak to us. He will use us to advance the Kingdom. With our senses alert and always switched on as we exercise ourselves in this, we can generate a life of posturing ourselves to listen and to watch. God will instruct us. Be encouraged, my friend, that in your diligence and willingness to be trained and 'drilled', the Lord will use you to bring transformation in the spirit to impact the natural wherever He places you.

How Do You Want to Use Me, Lord?

When military training is complete, there is a graduation or 'passing out' ceremony to acknowledge that one is now officially recognised as a soldier. When fully trained and armed, the soldier will be called upon to go into battle at a moment's notice. Similarly in the spiritual training God does with you, you should expect to receive your battle orders potentially with the words, 'This is your mission should you choose to accept it!' That was how it happened to me.

The question to ask now is, 'Where are You sending me, Lord and what is the assignment?' If you know you are at that place, ready to ask now, then why not ask this question of the Lord? Posture yourself and deliberately make yourself available through your prayers and heart response. If this is brand-new to you, you need to acknowledge the call to be trained and to respond to the Lord's call in your own way. It is time to be exercised and to understand your spiritual senses are weapons as well as gifts.

PRAYER

I pray for you as the Lord speaks to you now—prepare the way of the Lord over you and your life! Lord Jesus, prepare Your child for all You have planned. The influence in the natural and the spirit You have ordained—let this reader be trained and exercised in the spirit for that aim and goal. Holy Spirit, I pray for Your lead and guidance for this dear one. I pray for faith to rise and for boldness and confidence to come now to step into that which You have called my friend. There is a call to go further, go deeper with You, Lord, and I pray for this precious one whom You draw into the depths of the unseen realm here and in Heaven. Take Your child, Lord, and reveal Your great mysteries and revelations in Your timing.

I bless you to have the sensitivity in and of the spirit to move with God and His unction. To flow with His Spirit and move with Him wherever He leads you into the unseen realms and even geographically in the natural-seen earth realm. May you know God's lead and proximity in your days and your nights. May you be confident in your obedience and see the Kingdom of God advanced to His glory alone!

7

MAKE READY FOR WAR

'MAKE READY FOR WAR! BE BATTLE READY!', IS THE CRY OF Heaven!

As the angelic forces are postured in their battalions in the heavens, so too must we, the 'army' of God, be positioned on earth. The more we learn to operate in the unseen realm with the Lord's leading, the more He will use us in His Kingdom battle strategies. We were made to advance the Kingdom of God violently and with force. We were created to advance, occupy *and* defend all that the Lord has called us to. We need to pay particular attention to the training of our spiritual senses, to learn to discern, move and operate in the realm of the spirit. In that place the Lord will reveal His plans to us as we wait on Him while watching, listening and continuing to focus our spiritual senses on Him. The further we yield and submit in humility, the more that will be opened and revealed to us. We will be given the great and unlimited joy of being known intimately by the Lord and moving with Him.

Maintain your intimacy with Jesus always and without question. Make it your absolute priority above all others. Read the Word of God and know Scripture absolutely—this is of key importance. But don't just read about the relationship Jesus offers us in the Bible, engage and participate in it! As you spend time with Him, be aware of what Jesus is inviting you into at any given time. It is from that place of focus on Him and complete rest and peace in Him that we are then called to advance the Kingdom with Him, in His timings, in His way. Let us make Psalm 86:11 our continued prayer: *'Teach me your way, Lord, that I may rely on your faithfulness....'*

As we yield, giving the Lord full access to our lives, our yielding opens the door to more of Him and His ways. Our understanding and surrender are crucial to operating in God's full, unquestioned, unopposed authority—we are made ready for war. One of my life verses is James 4:7. Be encouraged to make it one of yours also:

> *Submit yourselves, then, to God. Resist the devil, and he will flee from you* (James 4:7).

We often hear people quote the second part of the verse and shout, 'Resist!', but forget to mention the essential first five words! Without our vital, intentional submission to God, we cannot effectively resist. The lower we go in humility before God, the deeper we move in God. The more we let go our control to come under His authority, the more we are released by Him to operate in it. In this, I believe, we are evermore trusted by God.

Emerging Warriors

God invites you to come out of your senses' training as a warrior and use the revelatory gifts you have been given to battle and win victory every time.

Scripture shows us the expanding leadership story of King David's life. His diligence and focus on God throughout brought advancement and increased his influence every time. We see David's story begin with him as a conscientious, caring and hardworking shepherd. He is dedicated in giving adoration and worship to the living God. We know this from his first response to the Philistine army in First Samuel 17:26, *'Who is this uncircumcised Philistine that he should defy the armies of the living God?'*

David knows God. He has worshipped the Most High, the living God, and trusted Him for a significant amount of time because his first response to Goliath's threat is who dares to speak that way to the Most High God's army?! Incredulous he moves, with his faith strengthened from time with the Lord, in this opportune moment to give God the glory He is due and to win against this enemy of the living God. David's life of worship and focus on God meant he was ready to go to battle at the exact times the Lord positioned him to do so.

In crucial moments throughout David's life story in Scripture, the Lord positioned David to be seen. He advanced him into the next level of influence for his life. From the sheep to the leadership of 'David's Mighty Men'—the incredible warriors with the same determination and gift for victory in battle as their leader—to becoming king of Judah and eventually king of Israel, David was prepared for each point of promotion through his devotion and diligence to the living God. He was faithful and

God was faithful to him. Let us posture ourselves in a life of worship, obedience and surrender to the Lord in the same way.

We see that David's killer victory combination of worship and warfare, adoration and battle success are synonymous with the man and his life. He was ever ready for war and advancement. He knew exactly what to do in the given moment of battle because he always sought out the Lord. We even learn from this king that when we move out from adoration in the living God into self-seeking and serving actions—as he did with Bathsheba—we can be quickly ensnared by sin and risk losing everything. Yet, if we stay close to God, defer to Him and His direction consistently, we will have victory and success in that to which God is calling us. That is the significant key—our battle strategy must be to hear when God has called us and do what He instructs, in His timing and with whom He calls us to do it. This is what enables success and victory, always.

I encourage you to read about David's exploits in the Books of First and Second Samuel and to meditate on these Scriptures. Ask God to reveal to you how David prepared himself in the unseen, secret place to advance the Kingdom. Read how every time David went to battle he sought the Lord for His strategy. He continually asked the Lord if it was time to go to war. Would he succeed? Each time he sought, the Lord answered and David was granted victory.

Out of time, isolated, making our own decisions—all these remove us from God and usually end in trouble and possibly disaster. King Saul, David's predecessor, demonstrated this well. We read of him acting out of time and order: he brought his own sacrifice to the Lord following the battle victory but without waiting for the prophet Samuel as he had been instructed.

Pride moved Saul out of kingship and into destruction. Let us learn from Saul and move with God.

So, where might we apply this spiritual truth in our own lives? To where is God calling you as your area of influence? Ask the Lord for His plan and strategy for advancement. Rest in Him daily. There is no need to panic and be in fight mode; rather, choose to rest in the Lord's closeness and move with Him as He is moving. We don't need to close our eyes tightly and get into anxious prayers. As we cultivate our relationship with the Lord, He will effortlessly reveal this to us as we ask Him how to move forward and advance.

Do you have a question about your work life, relationships, location of living, mission, ministry or finances? Whatever it is, meet with the Lord and He will show you the way through. If you are called spiritually to oversee a group of people, a region, town, city or nation, the same principles apply. Whatever your remit of influence is, watching and sensing with the Lord will always lead you into, not away from, His plans for your life and the advancement of His Kingdom through you.

DETERMINED COURAGE

Let us not shrink back through fear of getting it wrong! Let us press forward in boldness and confidence; be like Jonathan and his armour-bearer who, in First Samuel 14, engaged a group of enemy Philistines by climbing up a steep cliffside because they had a word from the Lord to do so! Jonathan, knowing the impressive loyalty of his young armour-bearer who would go with him anywhere, declared that if the adversary shouted from the garrison on the hill, 'Come up to us', he and his armour-bearer would go up and defeat them. Two against a whole army. The

Lord defeated the army because of two men's crazy, faith-filled courage. I absolutely love these two and their fearless attitude!

> *But if they say, 'Come up to us,' we will climb up, because that will be our sign that the Lord has given them into our hands* (1 Samuel 14:10).

Receive these supernatural warriors' boldness and courage and step into all the Lord has called you to. Know that He will show you the way, even in the most impossible-looking circumstances. Let us be those who run into battle with boldness and confidence in our God!

GOD WILL CALL YOU

Wherever you are and however you feel about yourself in this moment, the Lord will surely call you and lead you into the battles you were made to fight and win. We know from how God works that He finds His warriors wherever they are positioned, even if they are hiding!

There was time when the nation of Israel was literally hiding out due to enemy threats. The Israelites were living in caves in the land God had given them. This was because their harvest and animals were being stolen yearly by the Midianites and other Eastern people. Judges 6 tells us how these people came 'like locusts' and stripped the land of resources. In their desperation the Israelites cried out to God for a solution. God sent a prophet who spoke on His instruction: the Israelites had gone against God's word; they had worshipped the gods of the Amorites and now their enemy had a hold on them because they had not listened to God.

At the same time, an angel of the Lord came and sat under an oak tree. The landowner's son, Gideon, was busy threshing wheat in a wine press to keep it hidden, thus preventing it from being stolen. Gideon was threshing in a dimly lit rock hollow that was dug deep into the land. He was not on the threshing floor, even though it would have allowed the grain to 'catch the wind' and separate the chaff, because he would have risked being seen by the enemy.

God saw Gideon. *'The Lord is with you, mighty warrior',* the angel of the Lord announced—to Gideon's surprise. As he considered himself from the least of the tribes of Israel and was concealed from everyone, it is not surprising Gideon, in essence replied, *'Who, me?'* (See Judges 6:12-18.)

God found Gideon and He will find us all. The Lord knows exactly where we are, even if we are hiding or seemingly out of sight as Gideon was. If you feel you are 'the least', as Gideon did, know that the Lord Himself will call you to battle at your due time. He will find you and He will call you into your assigned battles with the assurance of triumph as you give your yes to Him.

Just as Gideon was called out as the mighty warrior he was to become, the Lord also has a plan for you to *'Go in the strength you have'* (Judges 6:14) to overcome your enemy together with God (see Judges 6:16). You will be given the strategy of the Lord to overturn your generational family altars and all limiting fears to lead others to victory! With abounding grace and patience the Lord will lead you through your uncertainties, questions and hesitations until you agree to His call to war.

JESUS, THE WARRIOR

We often think of Jesus being the quiet, gentle minister. However, Jesus Christ our God, as a man on earth, was a warrior in His every word, declaration of Scripture, healings, deliverances and perfect timing. He initiated the expansion plan of the Kingdom of God on earth by introducing and revealing the Gospel of the Kingdom and its outworking. The violent advancement and expansion of the Kingdom of God is war. There can be only one King and only one Kingdom! Jesus Christ, the Prince of Peace, the One who calms and stills the storm says in Matthew 10:34: *'Do not suppose that I have come to bring peace to the earth. I did not come to bring peace, but a sword.'*

Jesus came to use the sword against His and our enemy in Christ. We know that our only enemy is satan and his army. 'The dragon' attempts to rule through the advancement of his influence on earth. Yet Jesus Christ came to stop him and establish His own Kingdom rule. We are called to stand in Jesus' name with the power and authority we have in Christ and to take up our swords next to Him. Revelation 12 tells of the enemy being hurled out of Heaven and attempting to usurp the plans of the Most High God by chasing after the people of God. We are informed that satan was *'not strong enough'* (Revelation 12:8) to fight Michael and the angels and lost his place in Heaven. If even in his heavenly home satan could not hold his place, how much less can he hold his place on earth where we have been given governance?

Despite the fact we have ultimate authority and power in Christ, the enemy still wages war against us, we who hold fast to our testimony of Jesus.

Then the dragon was enraged at the woman and went off to wage war against the rest of her offspring—those who keep God's commands and hold fast their testimony about Jesus (Revelation 12:17).

Yet it is prophesied that we will be victorious and overcome *'by the blood of the Lamb and by the word of their testimony'* (Revelation 12:11). This is the killer blow. We overcome. Victory is ours in Christ when we do *not* shrink back but press forward into battle as our Lord leads us.

...they did not love their lives so much as to shrink from death (Revelation 12:11).

Death to self. Death to our own will. Death to our own agenda and preferences and rather fullness of life in Christ who leads us into victory. We must offer complete submission to His authority and no other. It is time to take up our sword for the Lord as did Gideon and his army! It is time to stand in the place of assurance of who our God is and the authority and power we have in Him through the application of spiritual gifts so that we can go forward together.

Jesus Christ is our Commander riding on His white horse! Revelation 19:11-16 tells us:

I saw heaven standing open and there before me was a white horse, whose rider is called Faithful and True. With justice he judges and wages war. His eyes are like blazing fire, and on his head are many crowns. He has a name written on him that no one knows but he himself. He is dressed in a robe dipped in blood, and his name is the Word of God. The armies of heaven were following him, riding on white horses and dressed in fine linen, white and clean. Coming out of his mouth is a sharp sword with which to strike down the nations. 'He will rule them with an iron sceptre.' He treads the winepress of the fury of the wrath of God Almighty. On his robe and on his thigh he has this name written: King of kings and Lord of lords.

This is our God! This is our King! Let us take up our sword for the Lord today!

RESPONSE

Lord Jesus, I choose today to take up my sword for You! I choose to battle and be on the offensive as You lead me. I desire to be like Gideon who was found by You and moved forward into battle together with You at the due time. I say yes to being used by You, God, to advance Your Kingdom mandate and see our enemy defeated. Use me, Lord, for Your glory!

SO WHO ARE WE ACTUALLY FIGHTING?

Seeing beyond the natural earthly realm and looking into the spirit realm enables us to see our true enemy. Having our senses fixed on the place the Lord has opened for us allows us to gain vital information from revelation about our enemy. The Lord will give us timings, approaches and detailed strategies.

Our enemy is never flesh and blood, never human beings in this context of spiritual warfare. It is always the unseen, invisible enemy to our natural eyes. We must look beyond the physical with our spiritual senses trained where God is directing to see and know our enemy.

> *For our struggle is not against flesh and blood, but against the rulers, against the authorities, against the powers of this dark world and against the spiritual forces of evil in the heavenly realms* (Ephesians 6:12).

God will open our eyes to see and to be aware of our enemy, to realise who is fighting *with* us and *for* us at the same time! The Lord illuminates the demonic and their plans as well as revealing His own. We may feel overcome or overwhelmed at this thought, but the Lord is with us.

One particular morning we were, as usual, worshipping as a team at GPA. The spirit realm opened and we saw a table of angels studying maps and plans on a table. The Lord revealed that this was a table for battle strategy for Scotland and the angels were focused on it. We prayed, asking the Lord to give us insight into this battle strategy so that we might partner with it. It was a determined, focused prayer, prophesying into what we were seeing and sensing in the spirit together.

Within ten minutes of speaking this prayer, we began preparing to write Lion Bites, our daily prophetic words. A couple of us were in the kitchen making coffee and, as we busied in the kitchen, there was a sudden shift in the spirit. My work colleague and I began to feel the movement physically. An almighty rushing sound increased and a strong anointing fell on us both. We began to shout and roar. This loud shout is familiar to us and is fairly common in God's intense presence, particularly in warfare and deliverance mode. Released by the Holy Spirit from me and others in our GPA team, it brings a breakthrough in the spirit or announces what the Lord is doing like a trumpet! The word for this particular shout in Hebrew is *ruwa*, the same shout that was released outside the walls of Jericho before they collapsed. The shout cannot be released at will, it is only discharged when the anointing forces it out!

Ruwa means to shout, raise a sound, cry out, give a blast. It is a war cry, alert or alarm of battle, signalling the march into war. It announces triumph, victory or joy. It also means a shout of destruction!

So, as we began to roar and shout, we knew that there was something significant happening in the spirit realm. Our bodies began to physically shake under the weight of the increasing anointing, and we could both see many angels rushing towards us in the spirit. Physical manifestations are common when atmospheric shifts occur in the spirit (see Acts 2). The Lord then spoke to me, informing me there was an angel who had just arrived in the worship room we had recently left. This was completely new for me at the time. I went, a little apprehensively, gently pushed the door open and peeked around.

As I looked into the room with my spiritual eyes sharply focused, I was shocked to see a man-sized angel standing in the middle of the room.

He was golden in colour, with a serious demeanour and was holding a scroll in front of him. He seemed to be waiting for something. Asking the Lord what I should do, as there was no protocol for angels showing up in the office, God told me to get Emma (Stark), our leader, and enter with her into the room. I duly went to fetch Emma and we went into the room, walking slowly to stand before the angel.

The angel began to read from the scroll about the battle strategy for Scotland. Emma received a scroll of words to eat just as we have read the prophets of Scripture did. In my case, the angel put his hand on my head, which literally threw me on to the floor with huge force. As he touched me, I received a download of many locations; I saw mountains, hills, rivers, waterways and much more. It was as if I were receiving a map of the nation in compressed visual form with key locations identified. My spirit received this revelation and held it.

We both sat on the floor for a long time and prayed that the Lord would lead us in His divine strategy and timing. Since then, God has led us in specific, on-the-ground prayers in many places in the nation. I have led teams up mountains, to lochs, coastlands, islands, rivers, towns and cities as the Lord has led, always in His timing and how He directs. It all began with this prayer and encounter with the Lord from the unseen spirit realm.

Had I not obeyed the Lord, had I shrunk back and not gone to see if the angel really was there, had we not engaged with the angel…we would not have received the revelation.

WORKING WITH ANGELS

Using our spiritual senses, we must learn to work with the angels as the Lord Himself leads us. We are used to seeing angels when we minister to individuals or groups of people and when praying in the spirit into a variety of subjects and often nations.

We see throughout Scripture that it is biblically normal to engage and interact with angels. We must not worship them of course, but we are given the model of men and women of God speaking with angels, receiving revelation and information from them both in the spirit (in the case of Daniel, for example) and in the earth realm, in the case of Mary the mother of Jesus, Gideon and others.

I encourage you to read Scripture and be attentive to the supernatural ways of God throughout, especially when angels appear and to note what their roles are. Men and women communicate with them to fulfil God's aims. It is not unusual to work with angels. It is a model we see played out time and again throughout the Old and New Testaments. Let us consider in Second Kings 6 what it looked like for the prophet Elisha, Elijah's disciple, to work with angels in battle.

The Bible tells us that Aram, leader of the Arameans, was furious with Elisha for constantly warning the king of Israel of Aram's battle plans. Aram made it his main purpose in life to capture him. Time and again the army of Israel avoided capture because Elisha heard in the spirit what the Arameans were planning. Aram, in a fury, came with his army to surround Dothan, where Elijah was. We read that Elisha was relaxed at this turn of events; we assume that this was because he already knew of Aram's intention in the spirit and he had insight by also seeing in the spirit. His servant, however, was not so relaxed about the scene outside the window at breakfast time!

> *When the servant of the man of God got up and went out early the next morning, an army with horses and chariots had surrounded the city. 'Oh no, my lord! What shall we do?' the servant asked. 'Don't be afraid,' the prophet answered. 'Those who are with us are more than those who are with them'* (2 Kings 6:15-16).

In this moment, Elisha prayed for the servant's eyes to be opened.

> *And Elisha prayed, 'Open his eyes, Lord, so that he may see.' Then the Lord opened the servant's eyes, and he looked and saw the hills full of horses and chariots of fire all around Elisha* (2 Kings 6:17).

Immediately, the servant saw in the spirit the angelic army of the Lord in their multitude. Amazing! What encouragement and security to see the Lord's army with you!

> *As the enemy came down towards him, Elisha prayed to the Lord, 'Strike this army with blindness.' So he struck them with blindness, as Elisha had asked. Elisha told them, 'This is not the road and this is not the city. Follow me, and I will lead you to the man you*

are looking for.' And he led them to Samaria (2 Kings 6:18-19).

The gift of sight that the Lord gave to Elisha and his servant was taken away from his enemies so that they would not win the victory they desired. We may find ourselves in a challenging situation, but we can also pray, 'Open my eyes, Lord, that I may see!' and we too will see and know the heavenly hosts who are for us and working with us. We can speak to the Lord knowing we can hear His instructions and pray in accordance with them. Perhaps, in time, we too will become as trusted as Elisha was when he asked the Lord to strike his enemy. The Lord will also back up our prayers!

Ministering Angels

Are not all angels ministering spirits sent to serve those who will inherit salvation? (Hebrews 1:14).

Angels come to minister peace and healing; they come to give revelation. They come to strengthen, direct, encourage and prepare us for that which the Lord has called us. In the Book of Acts, we read Paul's account of the angelic and how certain angels are assigned to us to outwork a particular service.

Last night an angel of the God to whom I belong and whom I serve stood beside me and said, 'Do not be afraid, Paul. You must stand trial before Caesar; and God has graciously given you the lives of all who sail with you' (Acts 27:23-24).

We are not alone in our work of advancing of the Kingdom of God. Angels belonging to God whom we worship and serve as Paul did will be sent to work alongside us as God ordains it. Our response here should be to acknowledge that our work with the Lord relies on partnering with the angels, like Paul, to be where God desires and instructs.

The God of the angels whom we serve with Paul is *Yehovah Tsebaoth* or *Elohim Tsebaoth*. This is one of the Lord's specific names in Hebrew which we see referred to in Scripture more than 285 times. This particular name means 'The Lord of Armies' or 'Powers' of both Heaven and earth, seen and unseen. This includes the angels as part of the hosts of Heaven. We know this because all the heavenly bodies were called the hosts of Heaven—in Hebrew צבא השמים *tseba hashshamayim*. God, in this context, being called the Lord of this 'host', showed that He is their Creator and Ruler. Therefore, in accordance with this name, we are reassured in what we know. We know that God Himself alone is to be worshipped—not creation. He is Lord of all 'hosts', planets, stars, the entire created order in the seen and unseen places.

As we realise and acknowledge our God is the Lord of angel armies and we submit to His authority in this, we become aligned with Him and those armies of angels. It then becomes easy for us to move with the angelic and work with them. He is our stronghold, and we will have victory in the fight. The Lord of Hosts is with us!

God is our refuge and strength, a very ready help in trouble. Therefore we will not fear, though the earth shakes and the mountains slip into the heart of the sea; though its waters roar and foam, though the mountains quake at its swelling pride. Selah. There is a river whose streams make the city of God happy, the holy dwelling places of the Most High. God is in the midst of her, she will not be moved; God will help her when morning dawns. The nations made an uproar, the kingdoms tottered; He raised His voice, the earth quaked. The Lord of armies is with us; the God of Jacob is our stronghold. Selah (Psalm 46:1-7 NASB).

PRAYER

We thank You, God, that You, the Lord of armies, are with us; in You we can never be shaken because You are our Stronghold, our Lord of Hosts who is with us as we align and submit to You and Your governance. Lord, teach me the ways of Your unseen realm! Open my eyes to see the angels You have sent to be with me in my work for the Gospel and the advancement of the Kingdom. Lord, let my eyes and senses be opened to see those You have sent to serve alongside me. Lord, I give You my eyes again and say anoint them afresh. Lord, enlighten them for Your service and the battle plans of Heaven. I submit to You, Lord, Captain of the Heavenly Hosts, to work with You and Your angelic army.

Allow me to see and know our enemy's strategies, Lord. Show me, illuminate Your plans and inform me how, when and where to battle in the unseen realm. Give me the wisdom of Your perfect timings and who is to fight with me that I may have victory in You.

NOTE: If working with the angelic is a new concept for you, may I suggest you study this subject further in Scripture. You can also find some helpful material on the study of angels; Tim Sheets has an informative book titled *Angel Armies* that I recommend, as well as further audio teaching on angels from Emma Stark at GPA. You could also consider joining our Prayer Institute training through the Global Prophetic Alliance, where we teach and train in much greater detail on the subject of spiritual warfare and strategic prayer, including working with the angelic.

8

The Key to Wisdom

God's opinion is paramount. We must seek Him for His opinion, His thoughts, His emotions and decisions about the things that are important both to us and to God Himself. We need to access His wisdom which is open to those of us who love Him.

It is impossible to access the realm of the spirit and God's wisdom through cerebral exercise alone. Learning, information and the knowledge we have is important and helpful in many contexts. However, wisdom from God and of the Spirit of God is not found in books or regular education. We cannot 'think' ourselves into the spirit or access it through exercising our brain capacity and mind. Revelation does not come through logical thinking. Analysis comes from the source of the Godhead in any form He chooses to reveal it to us. And the method of revelation can vary at any given time.

Perhaps we may find it through direct illumination of Scripture: visions; words of knowledge; prophetic instruction in words; dreams; signs and wonders; and, like many, we can read of it in the Bible directly through Spirit encounters and interaction.

'For my thoughts are not your thoughts, neither are your ways my ways,' declares the Lord (Isaiah 55:8).

Our education—in and of the spirit—comes from the Spirit of God Himself, the 'wonderful counsellor' Jesus Christ, who brings us into His wisdom and that of the Holy Spirit who guides us in His truth. If we desire truth, to know God's thoughts, ways and pure wisdom, we must be willing to open ourselves to encounter the Lord and His Spirit in any way He chooses and at any time. The expressions of revelation are multifaceted. God is the Creator, therefore always expect the unexpected in remarkable, creative ways that God may choose to speak to you.

We will miss revelation if we expect it to come only through reading the Bible or in visions or dreams thinking, *That's the way God always speaks to me*. Broadening our expectations and anticipating that the Lord will break in with His gift of wisdom through a variety of means is important. If our intellectual intention is to 'study' our way into the spirit realm and God's deep wisdom and mystery, we will always fall short. We must engage our minds *and* spirits with *the* Spirit.

Knowing the Scriptures in the Bible is absolutely key. Gaining understanding through them is essential for our education in the ways of the Spirit of God. We must always ask the Lord to illuminate His Word to us through our meditation on the Scriptures: they are central and essential to our learning and knowing the ways of God. We must absolutely value and nurture our understanding of Scripture without question.

> *Jesus replied, 'You are in error because you do not know the Scriptures or the power of God'* (Matthew 22:29).

Memorising Scripture is not knowing it. Learning the words does not mean we truly connect and grasp the fullness of their meaning internally. We can study Scripture and read commentaries; we can learn Hebrew and Greek; we can be the most intellectual, academic biblical scholars on the planet—and yet, in our studies, we may still not have completely grasped the spiritual significance of His Word. We may have missed the door of access to the Trinity directly in relationship through Christ. Great biblical scholars can be devoid of any belief in Christ Jesus at all.

Please know I am not decrying Bible study here. It is highly valued and is essential for all to understand the context and meaning of the Word of God. I encourage all to prioritise scriptural study and meditation daily. However, if we take reading the Bible in isolation, devoid from fully alive relational connection, we are falling short. The Bible gives us access to the Author, the divine nature and personhood of God, the Trinity. Relating intimately with the Source of the Word is vital to accessing our God who is Spirit and to the realms He has created and inhabits.

There is a spiritual 'deep dive' call from the Lord both into His Word, as Scripture, *and* into the Spirit of God. The realm of the Spirit is open to each person born again in Christ. It has a multifaceted, incredible, often indescribable beauty and layered meaning. This is what gives us understanding into the unfathomable nature of God and His ways.

We see and we know in part (1 Corinthians 13:9). Our aim should be to take the revelation and knowledge we have of the Lord and His ways and let it leave us burning for more. Staying hungry for more understanding of God and His divine nature ensures that we do not allow ourselves to settle for what we know already. *'Allow God to stir up your hunger and thirst for more of His righteousness and you will be filled'* (see Matthew 5, especially verse 6). Ask the Lord to stir your appetite for more of Him and He will surely do it.

> *...no one knows the thoughts of God except the Spirit of God* (1 Corinthians 2:11).

Truly 'knowing' the Word of God through meditating on the Bible can open us to the layered understanding given by the Spirit of God. It is when we can experience those light bulb *'aha'* moments of revelation in meditation. In addition, when we enter into the realm of the spirit to seek God in a deeper relationship, we come face-to-face with the actual revelation of the Word. We can be given understanding and revelation knowledge which will change us forever. This will enable experiencing Him and it in a multidimensional, full colour, fully alive way.

THE WAY TO WISDOM

My wish is that I could describe accurately and effectively the most profound and incredible encounters in the realm of the Spirit that the Lord has opened to me and many others. I could then invite you to step into them so that it would be easy for you too to experience the extreme, intense and overpowering nature of God and acknowledge that His ways are indeed marvellous and amazing.

This is such a challenge because it is like trying to write a Pulitzer Prize-winning description of the most intense, awe-inspiring sunset which will stay in a memory forever. I could not even begin to do that description justice. You would not feel the emotion I felt, engage in the full-sense experience that I did or feel its subsuming nature. However, I hope I can stir up your hunger to push through and open yourself up to more of God and His Spirit, for knowledge of Him and His wisdom. I pray for impartation to help awaken your spiritual senses as I have experienced this. I pray now that the Lord will open the spirit realm before you. I encourage you to enter into greater intimacy with the Lord which is never-ending. However, it is in cultivation of your desire and burning passion for more of Jesus Christ, the Father and Holy Spirit that will push you beyond your previous limits of encounter into the fathomless depths of the spirit realm.

> ...*The Spirit searches all things, even the deep things of God* (1 Corinthians 2:10).

There is always more. God is eternal and unrestricted in nature. There are always greater depths and new realms to encounter with the Lord. Greater revelation and more wisdom of His nature and Word. We will never be at the point of completeness in the knowledge of God or His Spirit in our lives on earth because of His eternal qualities.

Following years of becoming familiar with praying to the Spirit, advancing the Kingdom as the Lord led me to do with Him in a variety of contexts, encountering and working with angels and being aware of the demonic and deliverance, the Lord said to me very clearly, 'You must forget what you know. You must move now beyond the limits of your knowledge.' He made it known to me that this was the invitation to go beyond the 'edge' of reason—that I needed to reach the liminal edge of what I knew, to go into the unknown and find what was being revealed by God Himself.

This invitation is open to all—to move beyond our mental limits. He says to you now, 'Be prepared to move beyond what you know and understand in your own strength.' It took me a while to discern what the Lord meant by this. For many years I had been used to watching, sensing and operating in the spirit from the earth. I was practised at looking into and sensing the spirit realm as well as seeing from the heavens back to earth in the spirit. I was used to being shown expanses of the realms of Heaven.

But God said, 'There is more. Move beyond what you know.' I had no idea. I did not have the cognisance or the imagination to grasp the incredible and often indescribable depth and breadth of all that is available and open to us as *citizens of Heaven* who dwell on earth now (see Philippians 3:20 NLT). The fullness of the meaning of 'oneness with Christ' and what it actually means in the spirit to be truly 'in Christ' was not mine. I did not understand the manifestation available to us in the spirit and the remarkable ways of revelation in Christ. Leaving human, earthly understanding behind and moving ahead of what we know in the natural is essential. We must untether ourselves from the limits of our thinking boundaries that tell us 'This is how it is' or 'This is how I will always encounter God' to enable ourselves to walk into new depths and realms of God's wisdom and ways.

However, as it is written: 'What no eye has seen, what no ear has heard, and what no human mind has conceived'—the things God has prepared for those who love him (1 Corinthians 2:9).

This Scripture informs us that there are things, currently hidden from us that we have never thought of or could even begin to imagine, that God has prepared for us. The Spirit of God invites you now into the place He has prepared for you to access them.

There is more for each one of us, beyond what we have experienced, which has been 'set apart' for us as individuals. These new experiences and wisdom come from exploring the realms of the Spirit of God with Him. As one in the Spirit, we receive the thoughts and understanding of God; and we receive the language to explain the spiritual realities God has given to us. Just as it is written in First Corinthians 2:

The Spirit searches all things, even the deep things of God. For who knows a person's thoughts except their own spirit within them? In the same way no one knows the thoughts of God except the Spirit of God. What we have received is not the spirit of the world, but the Spirit who is from God, so that we may understand what God has freely given us. This is what we speak, not in words taught us by human wisdom but in words taught by the Spirit, explaining spiritual realities with Spirit-taught words (1 Corinthians 2: 10-13).

I encourage you to read and meditate on the full chapter 2 and pray it through as you do. For, as Paul instructs, there is a wisdom for the mature that comes from the Spirit. It is through acknowledging this reality and working with Holy Spirit as He leads us into the depths of His wisdom that we begin to access the fullness of it.

I explained earlier in this book about the need to exercise our gifts of discernment repeatedly so that we can become mature (Hebrews 5:14). As we begin and maintain a life of constant use of spiritual discernment, of activating our spiritual senses, then the fullness of who we are to all of who God is will enable us to mature and to be invited into the depths of wisdom with and by the Spirit of God.

As you meditate and consider First Corinthians chapter 2 further, please allow God to draw you into greater understanding of what it means to be mature in wisdom. Ask the Lord what is the *secret wisdom that has been hidden* and what God *planned before the world began* (1 Corinthians 2:7 ERV). Allow your hunger for understanding God's ways to increase and burn in you as you meditate on this portion of Scripture. This invitation for more is pressing on you now. Paul revealed that the secret wisdom reserved for you is accessible through the Spirit of God who *searches all things, even the deep secrets of God* (1 Corinthians 2:10 ERV). Imagine that for a moment—the Spirit of God moves through, accesses and mines the extraordinary volume of the profound, weighty expanses of God's mysteries, His secrets. Is that not incredible?

The Spirit of God reveals what God has given to us. The Spirit knows the thoughts of God and we will be taught these truths by the Spirit in spiritual words, which the Word of God says will only be understood by those who discern by the Spirit of God. Our spiritual receptors must be activated and focused to access this unearthly domain.

Let Us Go Deeper

We are armed with the understanding that we cannot enter the realm of the spirit if we are holding on to human wisdom, information and knowledge as our access point. We must release the weights of human knowledge and logic that may have tied us wrongly to the earth realm. As we choose to move beyond and into the unknown, we are assured God is with us. By moving into a place where we can say, 'I let go of what I know in my own strength and I step beyond into Your understanding and knowledge' we are brought to an incredible access point of the spirit. These phenomenal yet uncomfortable places will be where we become fully reliant on God and fully reliant on His ways because they are so unfamiliar.

See by the Spirit. Know and be informed by the Spirit. Move by the Spirit. Your goal is to know God more. We must come up and move past what we see and understand in the natural earth realm. We must look beyond, using our spiritual senses to gain the perspective of Heaven and understanding from the Lord. Wisdom may be hidden but it is not difficult to find when we ask God for it and pursue it. Wisdom through the Spirit is the key that opens the door.

Enlightenment by the Spirit

Begin by asking the Lord for the eyes of your heart to be enlightened (Ephesians 1:17-18). Allow your desire to know God better to increase through the Spirit of wisdom and revelation. Let us not become complacent or satisfied with our level of knowing God.

I keep asking that the God of our Lord Jesus Christ, the glorious Father, may give you the Spirit of wisdom and revelation, so that you may know Him better. I pray that the eyes of your heart may be enlightened in order that you may know the hope to which He has called you, the riches of His glorious inheritance in His holy people (Ephesians 1:17-19).

As we study the meaning of this portion of Scripture, we can see Paul is praying for us that we will know God better through the gift of the Spirit of wisdom and revelation. He uses the Greek word *apokalupsis*, meaning from its root word, 'the taking off the cover to disclose in light'. In verse 18, Paul prayed for our vision, imagination and mind of understanding to be illuminated. We know through reading Scripture that the gift of wisdom is highly prized. Those who seek and ask for wisdom are honoured and revered. Those who heard Jesus speak and teach while on earth were amazed at His wisdom and authority. He often spoke in a way that those with learned academic wisdom could not understand. Utilising parables in His teaching enabled Jesus to fulfil the prophecy of Isaiah 6 where not all would hear and see Him as God's Son.

The disciples came to him and asked, 'Why do you speak to the people in parables?' He replied, 'Because the knowledge of the secrets of the kingdom of heaven has been given to you, but not to them. Whoever has will be given more, and they will have an abundance.

Whoever does not have, even what they have will be taken from them. This is why I speak to them in parables: "Though seeing, they do not see; though hearing, they do not hear or understand" (Matthew 13:10-13; see also verses 14-15).

We comprehend from Jesus' explanation here that the only way we may come to have the wisdom of God and His Kingdom is through Jesus Christ Himself. No one can access the revelation of the Kingdom and of God without Him. Paul tells us that *all* mystery of God, treasure of wisdom and knowledge are hidden in Christ.

My goal is that they may be encouraged in heart and united in love, so that they may have the full riches of complete understanding, in order that they may know the mystery of God, namely, Christ, in whom are hidden all the treasures of wisdom and knowledge (Colossians 2:2-3).

How Do We Ask for Wisdom?

How often do we ask the Lord for His wisdom and insight into a situation? Have we always asked the Lord for the gift of wisdom as we are encouraged to do by the apostle James?

If any of you lacks wisdom, you should ask God, who gives generously to all without finding fault, and it will be given to you (James 1:5).

My sense is that if we were a people of God who always asked for His wisdom, our lives would look very different. Imagine if we requested God's wisdom and opinion in Christ for our relationship issues, family dynamics, work opportunities and conflicts. What might our world and life look like compared to how it is now? The Lord delights in us when we ask for His gift of wisdom. When we ask for some, the model is that He gives us more!

Solomon, the young son of King David, was destined to be blessed with favour and impact. God had promised David this. However, on being anointed king of Israel, Solomon chose not to rely on his own destined purpose which God had already prophesised into multiple times. He decided that he needed something of great value to fulfil his role with excellence. So he asked God for His wisdom.

> *So give Your servant a heart to judge Your people, to discern between good and evil. For who is capable of judging this great people of Yours?* (1 Kings 3:9 NASB)

God's answer?

> *Now it was pleasing in the sight of the Lord that Solomon had asked this thing* (1 Kings 3:10 NASB).

The words in Hebrew for an understanding heart are *shama leb*; used in the original text, we understand that Solomon asked for wisdom from God so that he would hear, understand and be obedient to that wisdom and that it would inform his heart, mind and emotions. Let us make this our prayer, my friend, that we may not only hear and sense God's wisdom but that we hear it, receive it and are obedient to it.

CHECK YOUR MOTIVES—COME WITH A PURE HEART

How do we check that we have wisdom from Heaven and are not being deceived? We can be sure that the opinion and wisdom of God is from Him if what we hear is as James outlines:

> *But the wisdom that comes from heaven is first of all pure; then peace-loving, considerate, submissive, full of mercy and good fruit, impartial and sincere* (James 3:17).

We can measure and test if what we hear and sense from the Lord fits this valuable checklist. Yet, if what we believe God says and this supports or reinforces our personal motives or intentions, then we need to reassess with urgency and ask the Lord for further confirmation! If we believe we have heard God but it is our human spirit speaking, then we will very quickly go off on a trajectory that moves us farther away from God's wishes for us or the situation we have been seeking Him.

Before we come to the Lord, let us lay down all our personal agenda, all motivations of our personal, human nature and ask for pure, clean hearts. If we come to the Lord laden with personal perspectives and hold on to our own understanding, if we take that baggage into the place of God's wisdom from the Spirit, then we will not hear and know God's voice clearly. We will be listening for what we want to hear. We will have revelation from the Lord, but with our own slant on it. We need pure, clean hearts, my friend.

Let us be like David who made this prayer regularly, *'Search me, O God, and know my heart: try me and know my thoughts: and see if there be any wicked way* [personal agenda/motive] *in me and lead me in the way everlasting'* (Psalm 139:23-24 King James Bible). Allow the Holy Spirit to convict us of anything that is prideful in origin, self-seeking or self-righteous; allow the light of Christ to illuminate our hearts and to penetrate the deep places of who we are, so that as God invites us to search Him and know Him, we approach with only righteous motives.

PERSONAL RESPONSE

Lord God, we desire to come to You as pure as we are able, for we know the pure in heart will see God (Matthew 5:8). We long to see You and know You. It is our desire for You to search and know us, Lord, to highlight any areas of our heart motivation that is contrary to You and Your ways, for we long to be ones who know You more, searching the depths of Your Spirit. Stir up the yearning in me even now, Lord, to desire more knowledge of You through Your Word and by Your Spirit. For I long to be more tangibly aware of the oneness I have with You. I long to know Your secrets and mysteries.

Search my heart, Lord. Search and know my motives. Convict me of any self-focus, self-serving attitudes and any darkness or wickedness in my heart. Convict me, Lord, of any area that needs to be brought before You, all the days of my life. I open myself to You now and I give You access to all of me. I ask now, Lord, that You show me the way of mature wisdom leading me to the place You have prepared for me.

Take time to sit with the Lord again. Be aware of the proximity of Jesus and speak to Him about what reading this chapter has stirred in your heart. Listen to what the Lord is saying to you. Watch His face and receive His adoration and love for you as He ministers and speaks into the areas He is highlighting. Go, with Jesus leading and allow Him to show you all He desires in this moment.

Bring the following questions before Him and allow them to help you begin a dialogue with Jesus. Take time to watch and listen between each question you ask Him; pay attention to how it feels. Go at a pace that allows you to be fully aware and completely immersed in the moment with your Lord without distractions. Allow Him to speak and show you all He desires in this time with you. Enjoy this encounter with the Lord.

- What would You like me to know right now, Jesus?
- What do I need to give You?
- What would You like to give or show me?
- What else do I need to hear or be shown by You today?

Do Not Rush the Revelation

Take time to watch and look. Allow yourself to ask questions of the Lord and all He is revealing to you as He shows you what He desires in this precious time with Him. Permit yourself time to linger. Do not rush through this exquisite, priceless time with Jesus—go with the tempo He sets. He loves you and longs to spend quality, uninterrupted time with you. This encounter of

Him and with Him will bring you more life and satisfaction than anything else on the planet.

Repeat this intimate experience as often as you can—if possible, daily. Be the person who saturates yourself in oneness with Jesus and allow Him to lead you where He chooses. Let Him love you and speak to you. Consent to His closeness in the spirit and in your emotions. You will see yourself transformed in the process. No one can heal like Jesus. No one else can reveal more of who He is than by allowing Him to lead you. He will introduce you more to the Father and the Holy Spirit. The realms of the Spirit will be opened to you further as you set aside time and focus for Him. There is more life for us in and by the Spirit of God than we ever dared dream or imagine. Begin this journey with Jesus and He will show you the way.

9

THE SECRET GARDEN

LET US SAY YES TO GOING DEEPER WITH THE LORD. LET US pray this psalm as we allow Him to draw us into a deeper relationship and the hidden, profound revelation. 'Teach us Your way, O God! Let us walk in Your way and never veer from it! We choose to go with You and follow You all the days of our lives.'

> *Teach me your way, Lord, that I may rely on your faithfulness; give me an undivided heart, that I may fear your name* (Psalm 86:11).

CULTIVATE THE WAY OF THE LORD

We need to become those who cultivate an ever-deepening personal relationship with the Lord and to allow Him to draw us in. Increasingly He will speak to us about many things and speak into so much more. Let our life testimony with Jesus, the Father and the Holy Spirit be one that has been shaped by many encounters. Let us experience the reality of the love and emotions of God, the feeling, seeing and savouring each time. This is my experience; and my prayer is that it will be yours as well.

I could not write of all of my encounters; there would too much to read and to comprehend. Many of these meetings with the Lord are so personal they cannot be shared. Some are intense, strange, unique and so prophetic in nature, speaking into both future and current events, that I must continue to process and speak to the Lord before sharing.

However, there are many occasions when God speaks and reveals His wisdom for other people and nations so that prophetic wisdom and knowledge from the Spirit can and must be shared. Words that affect life, family, individual, work choices, business, economic and governmental decisions and more. As we allow ourselves to be drawn into the greater knowledge of God, He shares His heart and opinion about many issues—those we prayed insight for and those we did not.

We need only a word of encouragement, direction, insight, healing or deliverance. Each time, the Lord knows exactly what we or someone we have brought before Him needs to hear, whether we or they realise it or not. He brings clarity and enlightenment, strategy and a road map ahead. There is a place where God speaks to us and we speak to Him. Jesus gave us the key to access this place when His disciples asked Him how they should pray:

> *But when you pray, go into your room, close the door and pray to your Father, who is unseen. Then your Father, who sees what is done in secret, will reward you* (Matthew 6:6).

The original language used for this place or room is *temeion*. So we know that Jesus is saying to come into the secret room, closet or place and to close the door. God is unseen in the invisible realm of the spirit, and we are praying to Him, unseen, from the secret place. This Scripture and teaching is also saying that, if we take time in the unseen place to pray, God Himself will see us and manifest a reward to us in an open, seen way.

There is a strong sense here in Jesus' description of setting ourselves apart in our meeting, conversational or contemplative prayer time with the Lord. As we intentionally set ourselves apart in a physical room and as we fix our focus on the Lord, we find ourselves aware of being one with the Lord in the unseen, internal, secret place *and* the unseen realm of the spirit. The Lord invites us again, 'Come to Me in the secret place.' The secret, closed place is where we 'lock in' with the Lord. It is the place from where we are to be motivated to position ourselves to pray. When we position ourselves in this intimate, hidden place with Jesus, our lives and those with whom we come into contact will never be the same again. The door is open to the secrets of God, His wisdom and His ways in this hidden place for us, my friend.

> 'Come and sit with Me in the garden.' Jesus invited me. 'I am giving you permission to sit here with Me and rest. Come. Sit down with me now.'
>
> I was given this prophetic word by a highly regarded, senior minister who was at a training weekend I was attending. He told me God had given him a prophetic word for me. This was, at that time, a completely new concept for me. Yes,

I talked to God. I knew 'listening prayer', I had impressions, visions, feelings and my senses were open in the spirit but no one had used the term 'prophetic' to me before.

The minister said, 'I am giving you permission to rest.' As he spoke these prophetic words over me, I saw Jesus. He was sitting under a huge, ancient oak tree at the top of a vibrant green hill. The vista from this high place was over many fields and hills; birds were singing and flying about the hedgerows. The warmth in the air and the gorgeous aromas of early summer were tangible. There was a picnic blanket laid out. Jesus was sitting on one side looking out over the view and clearly inviting me again to sit with Him.

As the minister spoke these words and I saw Jesus' invitation in the spirit, I broke down in tears. I was flooded with such overwhelming gratitude for being known and understood by my God. I cannot describe how lightened and relieved I felt. Emotional exhaustion had been underneath the surface for some time. I had been asking the Lord to give me help and direction for weeks—for Him to give me a sign for what to do. He spoke straight to my heart that day. I can recall the detail of the room, exactly where I was standing and the words used. That prophetic word changed my life forever.

If you have ever heard a prophetic word that hit the mark, you know how impactful it is. The person ministering, when speaking straight from God's heart into your situation, will pierce you with a bull's-eye hit! For many years in prophetic ministry we have delivered words from the Lord to those coming to us for insight and direction, bringing healing, freedom, confirmation and assurance. It has been our joy, honour and privilege to see people so built up and set free, overjoyed and to witness heavy burdens falling off them time and again. However, receiving that word for myself, years ago in that specific moment, was revolutionary.

As a family we had recently toiled through months of ugly pain and raw, heavy grief. Some months previously, our young goddaughter had died following a horrific, freak accident. The child's parents had been our close friends for years. They were as family to us. We had journeyed through pre-married life, marriage, pregnancy and our children growing up together. This tragedy broke so much in us, both individually and together as families, to the point that at times it was unbearable.

The night of the accident the Lord had revealed to me what would happen. We had rushed to be with our friends at the hospital as their daughter underwent extensive surgery. We waited hours together. I sat with them, praying and reading the Bible until the child was through major surgery. As I prayed, God gave me a shocking vision showing me that she was already dead and being kept alive medically by intubation. I chose to ignore the meaning of the vision. I thought I must have got this wrong because I could not understand why God would reveal the death of this darling child to me. Surely not, God?!

The word of the Lord then came to me, 'Let the little children come to Me.' I said, 'God, You can't mean that! How can this be? Surely she will live.' I moved past this and thought I must have misunderstood; God must be telling me something else about her salvation. I assured myself that, through this horror, there would be a testimony from Jesus to mean that she would live.

Five excruciating sleepless days and nights later we received the news that she was officially brain dead and her life support would be removed.

But God! We had prayed for a miracle together: so many people were praying. Privately in the ICU room, I had laid my hand on her right leg praying for her legs to move and dance again. I had whispered prayers of healing and hope in her ear and seen her brain activity monitors peak when I mentioned Jesus. I had reminded my goddaughter of conversations we had recently about Jesus and reassured her that He was with her. I didn't realise then that she would be with Him for eternity.

The pain of loss of a loved one is horrific. Pain of the loss of a child is beyond that. We supported our friends in their darkest times not knowing if their lives would survive this brutal loss. Simultaneously, my husband and I were processing our own pain and journey of faith with the Lord. But I could not pray. As in Psalm 88, I was disconnected from God and stuck in a removed place, not knowing how to move forward for long weeks after. Friends of faith stood with us. They prayed for and with us over weeks and months. Eventually the darkness became less bleak and light began to break in.

Immediately after my goddaughter's death I had told God I never wanted to see or hear another thing in the spirit if it was going to be so heavy a burden. Yet in God's kindness, He loved me and remained close to me even if I could not feel it at the time. Visions of this precious girl began to be revealed to me: I saw her dancing, twirling and spinning with such grace in the spirit. Jesus showed me that she was with Him and began to speak to me about her. Her mother had a dream where our girl was pointing to her right leg and saying, 'Tell Aunty Sarah-Jane about my leg.' Her mother did not know I had laid my hands on her right leg and said, 'Let these legs dance again, Lord!' When she told me of this dream, we were both overwhelmed by God's goodness and we cried with joy.

Much later, I saw Jesus pass a baby to her in the spirit. I heard the Lord say, 'Tell them there is a baby coming.' My friend had heard a voice tell her the same thing that week. Again we were overwhelmed. Some months later she became pregnant and had a beautiful child. This was a testimony of Jesus coming through in a way we never foresaw.

The ways of God are truly mysterious.

We cannot understand His ways. Especially when our human frailty cannot comprehend the stripping rawness, the baring and breaking of all that was assured before walking through the trial of our life. Previously I had prayed with such assurance, 'God, my faith in You is so strong I feel that nothing could change that—it feels so secure, unshakable.' Looking back at what then happened, the hymn 'Will Your Anchor Hold?' comes to mind. I had no idea such an experience would happen in our lives and that it would bring us so close to losing everything we had felt we had gained in Christ. To be with Christ in His suffering is something we often move swiftly past, even as those who love the Lord. Walking through death and pain brought us to such a place of shaking that we doubted we would recover from it.

But God.

The day that the prophetic word came to me, along with Jesus' invitation and permission to rest, changed my life. I was rescued from the limping pain of grief and loss; I was restored. This invitation to sit down with Jesus had taken me beyond everything I had previously known about Him and beyond all my knowledge of who He was before the accident.

I saw Jesus and wept. I sat down with Him and came into His rest.

Over time, I regularly sat with Jesus intentionally and let Him heal my brokenness. We talked and walked together. He brought wholeness where there had been devastation. He gave me strength and insight for the present and future. Being with Jesus in such a profound way gave me rest for my weary soul and hope for the future that had previously been covered with darkness.

Whatever you are going through or have been through, Jesus is there waiting for you to come to Him. He is offering a new beginning and refreshment with Him in that deep place of rest. He says, 'Come to Me all you who are heavy burdened...have rest for your soul.' The invitation from the Lord Himself to us comes from Matthew 11:28. In *The Passion Translation*, Jesus speaks the offer to us again:

Are you weary, carrying a heavy burden? Come to me. I will refresh your life, for I am your oasis. Simply join your life with mine. Learn my ways and you'll discover that I'm gentle, humble, easy to please. You will find refreshment and rest in me. For all that I require of you will be pleasant and easy to bear.

The original language Jesus used here says to each of us, 'Come and follow Me all you with heavy burdens and I will give you refreshment and rest. Be yoked to Me with ease and not weighed down by your heavy burden. Learn and understand from Me, for I am gentle, humble in my heart and emotions.'

Here is the key: Jesus tells us what we will find. The original Greek is *heurisko*, meaning to find and obtain a perspective of rest for our soul, life, heart. This is not a one-off invitation. It is a permanently open door that remains in place for all those who know Jesus and those who do not.

'Come and follow Me, enter My rest and sit down with Me'—I had been given the prophetic word to sit with Jesus and permission to stop. I took the word to heart and arranged an extended break from work to ensure a long sabbath with the Lord. Over the months I learned to listen to Him and see Him in a new way. Complete assurance that He was always easily available and accessible, with something always to give me and bless me, was built into me by the Lord. Such love and lifting is available to us all! 'Come to Me' Jesus says. 'Come to Me, again and again. Never stop coming to Me.' The challenge is to maintain that place of rest with Him and not to push ourselves away. We should move ourselves towards Jesus and His gentle heart.

THE DOOR IS OPEN TO THE SECRET MEETING PLACE

As a child, one of my favourite books was *The Secret Garden* by Frances Hodgson Burnett. It is the beautiful tale of orphan Mary Lennox. She finds herself removed from her home in 19th-century India following the death of her entire household. Deposited in her unknown uncle's care on the edge of the wild Yorkshire moors, she only has access to two rooms in his large, cold mausoleum of a house. The housekeeper instructs her to go out into the extensive gardens to keep herself occupied.

The child's solitary exercise leads her to discover a door to a walled garden that has been locked up. Her uncle's late wife had loved this secret garden. Since her death, the story tells, he could not bear to go inside and had forbidden access to all. Mary, however, finds a way in and so begins the story of both a restored garden and restored childhood. We see how relationships and hearts are healed through the bringing to life of the secret garden with the help of the two boys with whom she becomes friends. The cultivation of the plants and restoration of the garden releases the beauty again. In this flourishing environment the children and the adults are allowed equally to come alive, blossoming and creating an ecosystem of emotional healing and vibrant life.

> And the secret garden bloomed and bloomed and every morning revealed new miracles.
> —Frances Hodgson Burnett, *The Secret Garden*

The 'miracles' we read about in Frances' famous novel are to be found in the secret garden of meeting in the spirit with Jesus Christ. Life flourishes when we meet with Him there. Once we have found the door of access we are compelled to return, time and again, because it is so filled with life and healing for us. Why would we stay away? We will find our senses burning with the love for Jesus. The fragrance and beauty of the garden into which He invites us are unique and perfect. By unlocking pain and hurt, He is restoring and strengthening us into renewed versions of ourselves.

'Come to Me you who are weary and find rest. Come and sit down with Me', the Lord says to you today. As we intentionally come to meet Jesus, we find ourselves in a secret place in the spirit that He has prepared to meet with us alone. We do not find it filled with other people. It is exclusive to Jesus and us. Your secret garden with Jesus will look different from mine and others'—it is perfectly designed because it is *your* garden. This is because we are meeting Him inside the secret place within— 'Christ in us the hope of glory.' We meet with Him in the intimate place deep within us.

We can see Jesus in various places in the spirit realm. In the place we are—home, work, outside—when we ask, 'Where are you right now, Jesus?', our senses will open to know and see and feel His presence. He is seated at the right hand of the Father so we can see Him in the heavenly realms as the Lord chooses to reveal Himself to us there. There are multiple places we can meet with Jesus, yet the secret inner place is, for me, the most precious and beautiful. It is the place that brings healing and wholeness to us which is so precious and intimate. From here the Lord takes us where He desires; He reveals more of who He is and brings healing to our personal brokenness. When our spiritual senses are attuned, we experience all of who He is and all that He has prepared for us in our relationship.

We read about the garden of intimacy in the Book of Song of Songs in Scripture. There are three chapters about love language and the appreciation of another's beauty, culminating in increasing desire for each and building to the moment of meeting in the garden. This book of love was considered so suggestive that, historically, only mature Jewish students were allowed to read it. The entire book is a passionate love story of desire that burns for love that is never satisfied.

We are introduced to the garden of meeting in Song of Songs chapters 4 and 5. This is the place of fruit and multiplication. It is the place of eating and drinking, fellowshipping in private, of intimate love. The garden is the place we see Jesus—as the one who is both called and named Himself the Bridegroom and who is acknowledged as the 'lover' in this context— meet with His Bride the 'Beloved'. Notice that it is the Bride's garden where He meets her; it is not His garden that she goes to. We hear the Bride say to her lover:

> **She/Beloved:** *Awake, north wind, and come, south wind! Blow on my garden, that its fragrance may spread everywhere. Let my beloved come into his garden and taste its choice fruits.*
>
> **He/Lover:** *I have come into my garden, my sister, my bride; I have gathered my myrrh with my spice. I have eaten my honeycomb and my honey; I have drunk my wine and my milk* (Song of Songs 4:16–5:1).

Earlier, in Song of Songs 4:12, we see the Beloved and Jesus say to her, '*You are a garden locked up, my sister, my bride; you are a spring enclosed, a sealed fountain*', much like the garden in the novel, waiting to be discovered and released into bloom. There is life in your garden. There is greater life and flourishing to come to you. The garden is an analogy for the spiritual place of cultivation. *God, the Gardener who tends the vines, is the One who tends you* (John 15:1). Jesus is the vine and we are the branches, growing as one, in and through Him. He says in John 15:5:

> *I am the vine; you are the branches. If you remain in me and I in you, you will bear much fruit; apart from me you can do nothing.*

'Remain in Me and I in you.' Come back to the secret place of meeting, over and over, and never leave. There is so much life for you there. Of course God's original intent as the Creator who made us, was to be in fellowship with Him in the garden.

We are truly made and designed by God to live with Him in the garden. We are now called back there—called to fellowship with Him in a new way.

As we choose to set ourselves apart to meet with Jesus, we will be led out of the difficult, desert places, leaning on His arm (Song of Songs 8:5). Love and desire that burns for Jesus cannot be awakened in advance of its time (Song of Songs 8:4); yet we can position ourselves to meet Him and allow that ache of yearning for Him, in the core of our beings, to be stirred. Let us take time to join with Him now, responding to His invitation to the secret garden of meeting.

Carve out some quiet and significant time, listen to instrumental worship music. Allow yourself time to respond to His invitation you have heard afresh. Choose to move towards Jesus in the place of meeting. Choose now to enter the secret place. Allow your heart and spirit to respond to Him in the way you are feeling drawn. Release your words to Him.

PRAYER

Jesus, I long to meet with You in the garden of my life, in the hidden secret place. I pray to You who dwells in the secret place of our gardens, let me hear Your voice! (Song of Songs 8:13) *Lord, I long to meet You there and spend time with You. I respond to Your call to 'Come and follow' You to the secret place where my burdens are laid down and I yoke myself to You. I long to enter the oasis of rest You are offering me and allow You to place Your ease upon me. I say yes to Your invitation and push the door open to the garden of meeting. I come to You now, Jesus, and ask You to open my eyes, ears and full senses to experience You in the place of rest. The hidden place within. Lord Jesus, would You show me this place that is exclusively ours to meet in together? I long to experience it with You.*

As you acclimatise your spiritual senses, engage your sight, hearing, smell/taste receptors and emotional and physical feelings with Jesus in the garden of your life. Ask Jesus to show you your personal spiritual garden and allow you to see Him there.

What is Jesus wearing? What is His expression and heart towards you? Feel His emotions of love. Take note of what the garden looks and feels like. Permit your senses to awaken to another level. (Holy Spirit, I pray for an increase now of this dear reader's sensory experience with You in the secret place).

Is it lush like a jungle? Does it look like an English country garden or desert oasis? Is it more like a children's playpark or a wild uncultivated landscape? (Everyone's spiritual garden and secret meeting place with Jesus is different and unique.) Take time to marinate your senses in what you are witnessing. Allow yourself to be completely submerged and saturated in the scents and atmosphere as you gaze around you.

Notice where you are positioned in the space and where Jesus is in relation to you. Watch Him and see what He is doing, saying, inviting you to do with Him. What is the Lord desiring to release and impart to you in this precious, bespoke environment?

If you wish, you can make notes in your journal after you have experienced this. You can see other parts and from other perspectives as you enter into dialogue with Him. Some helpful questions you can ask to begin the conversation:

- What would You like to speak to me about, Jesus?
- What do You want to give or show me here, Jesus?
- What would You like me to give You, Jesus?
- What do You think about..., Jesus? (Insert any subject about which you wish to ask His opinion)

Speak to Jesus and converse as friends, for God is our Friend. God spoke to Moses as a friend and God calls us to be in friendship with Him. We do not come to the garden as servants but as friends. We do not come asking, 'What can I do for You, God?' We come to be one with Him and to speak as friends and beloved ones together.

> *No longer do I call you servants, for a servant does not know what his master is doing; but I have called you friends, for all things that I heard from My Father I have made known to you* (John 15:15 NKJV).

Ask the Lord how often you may come and meet with Him here. Gain the assurance you need from Him to ask any questions you may have. Frequently, in these secret garden times, the Lord will reveal particulars of our lives. As the Gardener, He will bring things to our attention and ask us to work through specific areas with Him, such as healing and freedom. The main purpose, however, is simply to be with Him and receive His deep rest. Enjoy repeat visits to this flourishing place and join with your Lord as often as you are able.

ARE YOU CALLED TO BE A VOCATIONAL DWELLER IN THE SECRET PLACE?

We are all called to the intimate place of meeting with the Lord. This is our inheritance as His Bride on earth. Yet some are called to enter into a repetitive permanent-type retreat with the Lord. We are drawn to experience extended times of sitting with Him in the secret place. Some are called to spend their entire lives focused on Jesus, the Word of God and to cultivate intimacy with Him all hours of the day or night.

Holy men and women, the 'Desert Fathers' and others similarly called in world church history, have been invited to give over their whole lives to spiritual husbandry with the Lord. There are many lives we can look at and see how God drew them in to a life of devoted oneness with Him: Brother Andrew; St. Teresa of Ávila and St. Catherine of Siena immediately come to mind. We see their lives manifesting the miraculous outworking of a human life conjoined with Christ. Incredible miracles of physical levitation in the glory of God are one such manifestation. This reminds us of the transfiguration of Christ when He was lifted up in the physical manifestation of the glory of God.

These are the days when God is calling His entire Body into that tangible oneness. He will bring forth His signs and wonders as He desires. We may not have every hour of every day to devote to secret place time with the Lord, but neither did those well-known lives, those who served and worked as well as who developed and enriched their secret place. Opening up to a tangible union with the Lord can increase despite our workloads and busyness. We can train ourselves to focus our internal gaze of emotions and our senses and meditations upon Him during our days and nights. Obsession, as King David wrote in the psalms, is constantly thinking of the Lord throughout the watches of the night with our thoughts continually returning to Jesus. We can touch Him and reconnect in the inner room with our emotions and mind throughout our days. Experiencing the lordship of Christ in an intimate way brings transformation to ourselves and those around us.

Be hungry for Jesus. I hear the Spirit of the Lord say, 'Allow Me to stimulate your passion to a burning desire for the Lover of your soul. Will you allow Me to burn you with the fieriness of love?'

> *Place me like a seal over your heart, like a seal on your arm; for love is as strong as death, its jealousy unyielding as the grave. It burns like a blazing fire, like a mighty flame. Many waters cannot quench love; rivers cannot sweep it away...* (Song of Songs 8:6-7).

The more we activate our spiritual senses to look and feel for Jesus, the more we will become aware of Him. He will be a tangible part of our lives daily. 'Where are You, Jesus? What are You doing now? I want to see You, Lord, and feel You close.' Let yourself become lovesick for Jesus just like the Bride who is almost driven to distraction by Him in the Song of Songs.

POUSTINIA

The Russian word *poustinik* describes someone who cultivates the secret place with the Lord to another level. The name of the place where they reside has its roots in the Russian *poustinia* or 'desert'. It is from the desert we come out 'leaning on our beloved.' The *poustinik* does not only go to a secret room at home but takes the secret place out of home to serve people in a new community. He or she builds a simple hut on the outskirts of a village or town. The community is honoured and blessed by this recognition as they know holiness is the *poustinik's* aim, feeding on the Word of God and prayer. Comprising one room, the shack includes a table and benches, fireplace and a simple bed. No lock is ever needed on the door because everyone is always welcome—along with Jesus—to the *poustinia*.

Days are spent reading the Word of God and in devotional prayer. They meet and listen to the Lord as they meditate on the Word, until they are required. Possibly someone from the village or town they are serving will ask for help with the harvest; perhaps someone is ill and they need support and/or prayer. Food and drink are always offered to the one who comes. The *poustinik* leaves home only with bread and salt to share. The food is a sign of the old and new covenant in Christ.

This surely is the picture we should hold before us—the way of the *poustinik*. Can we be one of those who are in union with Christ in a quantifiable way and for those we live amongst? Are we ones who dwell so deeply in the Word and in union with Christ that we are ready to go and serve those to whom we are called?

A life that is one with Christ but spent locked away in a room without community is not a life representing the life of Him within. From the secret place comes fruit and flourishing. Where has the Lord asked you to flourish and bring fruit? Perhaps it is time to meet with Him again in the garden and ask the question of Jesus.

10

EXPERIENCING
THE IMPOSSIBLE

*At first people refuse to believe that a strange
new thing can be done, then they begin to
hope it can be done, then they see it can be
done—then it is done and all the world
wonders why it was not done centuries ago.*
—FRANCES HODGSON BURNETT,
The Secret Garden

THE REALM OF THE SPIRIT IS OPEN IN A NEW WAY TO YOU
today. It is time to go deeper and further with Father God, Jesus
and the Holy Spirit into the greater reaches of His mysteries and
expanded experiences. Access is open. Let us enter and reflect
what is currently unseen of God in the earth realm.

REFLECTING THE UNSEEN

God chose a people to reflect who He is on earth. The supernatural God uses supernatural ways to reveal Himself through His people. In Acts 6, Stephen saw and experienced the Lord in Heaven in such a way that it led to the people watching him to believe he was an angel. They saw the illuminating light of the glory of God radiating from Stephen's face, as it did centuries before with Moses. How did Stephen, apostle John, Isaiah, Ezekiel and Daniel all see the Lord in His blinding, pure and brilliant glory, seated on His throne, burning eyes of fire and holy white purity?

They saw His form in holiness with their eyes open from the earth realm into the spirit realm. These holy men experienced and reflected the beauty and glory of God from the unseen realm as they stood in the earth realm. We know they had pure hearts because those who have pure hearts will see God (Matthew 5:8). The Lord revealed Himself in His spotless, burning, brilliant holiness during challenging and dark times, times of persecution and false god and idol worship. Today, the Holy One is again revealing Himself to many by His Spirit. He allows us to see Him as He is now, reigning in glory seated on His throne. He is calling for purity in us so that we may see Him and reflect His beauty. All honour, all glory is His. For He is worthy and only He is holy.

Meditate on God's holiness and allow yourself to begin to worship Him for who He is and always has been. Take time to glorify and honour Him from your own heart. There is one King on the throne over all nations, seated in authority above all peoples; He created everything that is in the seen and unseen realms. He is Lord and He is holy.

The Lord calls us, His church on earth, to position ourselves at this time to be the ones who see and reflect His glory, just as the men as revealed to us in the Bible did: to see Jesus at the right hand of God; to witness the Lord with the train of His robe filling the temple; to be elevated by the reality of God's glory today as we live on the earth. As we see Him in His holiness and purity, we recognise our lack and cry out to God in our unclean state like Isaiah did (see Isaiah 6). Allow His holy conviction to take you to the place of burning and purification by His Spirit, for He alone is worthy, pure and spotless. Keep coming back to gaze upon and meditate on the Lord's holiness and you will be transformed, seeing more of Him reflected in more of you.

We must be, as in Isaiah 60:1, the people who *'Arise, shine, for your light has come, and the glory of the Lord rises upon you'* in a world covered in deep darkness. The light of the world in its actuality is shining on us for all to see. Radiant pure light released from us is not only witnessed in the unseen spirit realm but in the seen earth realm! That burning, white, living light will come to rest upon us individually and corporately so that we become the *'city on a hill that cannot be hidden'* as Jesus spoke of in Matthew 5. The city of light will manifest in us and through us. It will be a tangible, literal manifestation of that light—not in some ethereal analogy but in actual reality so that many people from all nations can run to and become one with the Light of Life that is Christ Jesus Himself, *'the light of the world'!* (See John 8:12.)

WHO WILL REFLECT THIS GLORY LIGHT?

The call is to us all. In Acts 6 we read about Stephen, whose name means 'to crown'. We know a significant detail about him, detail that is given to few followers of Jesus in Scripture. We read that he demonstrated a life of purity and holiness, one who exhibited the Gospel of the Kingdom.

> ... *They* [the apostles] *chose Stephen, a man full of faith and of the Holy Spirit.... Now Stephen, a man full of God's grace and power, performed great wonders and signs among the people* (Acts 6:5,8).

Opposition to Stephen's words rose up from the learned Jewish teachers and yet Acts 6:10 informs us, *'they could not stand up against the wisdom the Spirit gave him as he spoke.'*

The grace, power and wisdom of God manifesting through Stephen provoked outrage. Lies were told about him speaking against Moses so that he could be brought to trial in front of the Sanhedrin, including the soon-to-be apostle Paul, who witnessed the whole thing (Acts 8:1). In this place of persecution they saw that Stephen's *'face was like the face of an angel'* (Acts 6:15). The original word for *face* here means also 'countenance' or 'person', so we can take from this they were mesmerised by his appearance being like that of an angel. We can imagine the luminescence radiating from him.

Stephen pronounces the testimony of Jesus from Abraham throughout Jewish history thus reminding the teachers of their story as Israel, God's people. Then:

> *Stephen, full of the Holy Spirit, looked up to heaven and saw the glory of God, and Jesus standing at the right hand of God. 'Look', he said, 'I see heaven open and the Son of Man standing at the right hand of God'* (Acts 7:55-56).

Stephen saw the Lord at his point of death. It was in the death of King Uzziah that the prophet Isaiah saw the Lord, as both Daniel and Ezekiel did in times of trial and testing when Israel was exiled to Babylon (see Isaiah 6). Apostle John, personally exiled to Patmos by the Roman Emperor, saw the Lord and great revelations of Jesus in and from the realm of the spirit.

What personal trial is upon us now? What might need to die in us for us personally to witness the Lord seated in His glory? For in our death we will see the Lord in His splendour. Where might God call us to live through a life of 'death to self' over His will being done in us? Are we willing to go there with Him and allow the Spirit of God to lead us so that we may radiate His glory?

Something in us has to die before we see the Lord in His glory and reflect His nature on earth!

Obedience, holding fast to the Word of God and yielding to His Spirit—whatever it takes, God! Whatever it costs or might look like, I am Yours! This level of death-to-self in time makes us a resting place for the Lord, the place where He will rest and reflect His glory upon us. Stephen's speech before his death culminates in the question to those witnessing his death, and it resounds afresh to us today as we look to Him—where will God rest on earth?

> *However, the Most High does not live in houses made by human hands. As the prophet says [in Isaiah 66:1]: 'Heaven is my throne, and the earth is my footstool. What kind of house will you build for me? says the Lord. Or where will my resting place be? Has not my hand made all these things?' (Acts 7:48-50).*

God is looking for a place to rest. Who will become that place of rest for the living God? Surely our response must be, as ones who now cultivate the place of intimacy with the Lord, 'Choose to rest Yourself on me, God, we are the ones who have made our rest with You.' As we dwell with God, He makes the sealed fountain of the Song of Songs' garden within us burst forth and become a river. The river represents the flowing of the Holy Spirit within. It is released to provide water not only to ourselves but those around us. Our cup is overflowing and saturating those who are parched in the desert as we once were. The way of the river of God from the fountain within will transform regions and lives.

We must see that this deep intimacy into which the Lord invites us is not just to activate our senses so we can enjoy more of Him. There is joy: however, the goal is to bring transformation to individuals, families, communities and nations from that proximity to the Lord. As we become the 'living body' of Christ fully alive in Him, the river of life will water the parched people and territories in our nations. By the Spirit of God we will be transformed. Through the Spirit of God, many will be saturated in and from the river which is overflowing from those joined in the Lord. It all begins in the intimate place of meeting, where we let go of our will and cling to God's alone. We die that we might live.

The invitation to us is to come, then to dwell in that place of meeting with the Lord. The more we intentionally abide, rest in and with Him, the more we see and sense Him. Jesus Himself is the gateway to the Father, the access to the fullness of the Godhead and the unseen spirit realm They inhabit. It is the way of life and the fruit. Again, let us read and absorb this truth Jesus reveals:

*Remain in me, as I also remain in you. No branch
can bear fruit by itself; it must remain in the vine.
Neither can you bear fruit unless you remain in me. I
am the vine; you are the branches. If you remain in me
and I in you, you will bear much fruit; apart from me
you can do nothing* (John 15:4-5).

Joined in Christ. Remaining and abiding in Christ. One
with Him. Let us be intentional about nurturing and experiencing this oneness. It is the way of the Lord and an ancient way
that is being opened to us afresh.

THE WAY OF THE ANCIENTS

During this ongoing journey of growing intimacy with the
Lord in my own life, He began to speak to me about the depths
of relationship available to us through Christ. He opened an
invitation to walk with Him in a new way. Seeing, sensing and
becoming increasingly familiar with the spirit realm, the draw
and pull from the Lord grew stronger the more it revealed itself.
It will come to you also, my friend, as you continue to pursue
greater depths of relationship with the Lord for yourself and
allow your desire for more of Him to increase. I heard the Spirit
of the Lord speak to me while sitting quietly with Him on one
of these occasions:

It's time for the new! Be open to the new! Take off
the old clothes of prayer and put on the ancient
ones. Put on the ways of Enoch and the ancients.
Walk in his path; walk in the ways of Enoch my
son. For it is time to watch as Enoch watched and
walk as he walked.

We are all being called back to the ways of the God who is the Ancient of Days in this hour. The new ways and paths we are being called to walk in are those trodden by the ancients of Scripture. We are called to walk the ancient path and follow those who went before us. We read of Enoch in the Book of Genesis 5:24, *'Enoch walked faithfully with God; then he was no more, because God took him away.'* We know, from the Book of Jude, that Enoch was the seventh generation from Adam—a number representing perfection. His name means 'trained and vowed; dedicated; profound'; so we understand that Enoch was trained and dedicated to walk with God. There was a focus and diligence to his walk with the Lord.

We know from reading Jude further that Enoch prophesied about the Lord's coming with His holy ones to judge everyone and convict the ungodly (Jude 1:14). He walked with God and prophesied what he heard and saw. Hebrews 11 informs us that at the end of his life on earth, Enoch did not experience death and was taken to the Lord, perhaps similarly to the prophet Elijah who was taken from the earth by the chariots of God and not through death.

There are only three men who Scripture acknowledges walked faithfully with God: Enoch, Levi and Noah. Levi was the father of the Levite priest tribe—a man, God says in Malachi 2:6, who spoke *'True instruction…and nothing false. He walked with me in peace and uprightness and turned many from sin.'* Noah, we read in Genesis 6:9,22, *'walked faithfully with God'* and *'did everything just as God commanded him.'* Oh may we be ones who do everything God commands of us! As the great grandson of Enoch, Noah was chosen to realise God's plan of hope and redemption for the earth through the Ark because he walked in faithfulness with God.

When we hear the Lord say to us that the new way of prayer and relationship with Him is actually the ancient way of these ones who walked with God, we must respond to that call. We must take off the ways we have understood prayer and relationship with the Lord to this point and be willing to pursue the ancient paths of walking faithfully with God that are now open to us.

There is no manual to purchase and read that tells us *how* to walk the ways of Enoch and the ancients. There is, however, an open gateway through Christ Jesus, and there is an invitation to walk with the Lord and be led by Holy Spirit. As we choose to enter through this open door of faithful, diligent intimacy, we are taken into this ancient way. God is revealing Himself to us in a way we have never experienced before. Prophetic insight and wisdom, understanding and counsel from the Lord is coming to us from this ancient path.

INTO THE UNKNOWN

To take off what we know of prayer and intimacy with the Lord and put on the way of the ancients is to move past what we know. It is to put ourselves into an uncomfortable place of moving and seeing beyond what we have already understood and accepted as truth. It is for us to become those willing to be led by the Lord into a liminal place—living on the edge with the Lord, if you will, pushing ourselves past the familiar and the certain into the place of revelation and illumination by the Spirit of God. We must be ready to move from the truth in Scripture and dive into the place of greater knowledge and revelation that is available to us. We must be willing to make ourselves available to being led by the Lord into the place beyond our current understanding.

These are the days of moving beyond understanding into the unknown.

BEYOND OUR PRESENT KNOWLEDGE

Revelation has been given to the people of God at different times in history through the illumination of God Himself. In Second Peter 1:12 (NKJV), we hear Peter speak of the *present truth* that has been revealed to him and exhorting the reader to be established in it. We read Paul, in Ephesians 3, further unpacking this reality of *present truth*—the perspective that truth comes to the people of God in different generations. In this case the revelation that Gentiles—not only the Jews—have full access to the Gospel of the Kingdom.

> *That is, the mystery made known to me by revelation, as I have already written briefly. In reading this, then, you will be able to understand my insight into the mystery of Christ, which was not made known to people in other generations as it has now been revealed by the Spirit to God's holy apostles and prophets* (Ephesians 3:3-5).

We know from church history that our understanding has changed through present truth revelations. Throughout the centuries clerics, such as Martin Luther in the 16th century, received insight from the Holy Spirit that salvation can only be gained by faith and not works. Others in church history have grasped an illuminated understanding of the living Word and apprehended it changing their and others' lives forever. They include John Wesley and those who formed new movements from that revelation such Baptists and Pentecostals.

All moves of God received the fresh present truth revelation from the Word of God which has reshaped our understanding of this.

Fresh revelation and present truth are found in the liminal place as we press forward into the 'as one' space with the Lord to experience His mysteries, just as Paul did. We are in the new era. Fresh revelation of the Word of God is coming to us at a pace by the Spirit of God. Choose to go beyond what you know and put yourself on the edge. Trust that God will reveal, in His due time, what is to be seen and heard.

THE LIVING WORD

The Word of God is alive and active (Hebrews 4:12). Jesus Himself is referred to as the Word made flesh. We are told the Word of God itself has life. By reading the opening verses of John, we can recognise the mystery attached to the Word:

> *In the beginning was the Word, and the Word was with God, and the Word was God. He was with God in the beginning. Through him all things were made; without him nothing was made that has been made. In him was life, and that life was the light of all mankind. The light shines in the darkness, and the darkness has not overcome it* (John 1:1-5).

The eternal, ever-present spoken Word of God has life that is eternal. God spoke His word and the heavens were made (Psalm 33:4), for in Him, all things visible and invisible were made.

> *For in him all things were created: things in heaven and on earth, visible and invisible, whether thrones*

or powers or rulers or authorities; all things have been created through him and for him (Colossians 1:16).

There is an invitation to encounter the living Word of God who is embodied in Christ Jesus afresh.

On one particular occasion, the table the Lord brought me to was alive with a bright white light. This was new. As I watched I began to see the 'living word' of God move across the table in front of me: moving at speed from left to right, page after page of writing passed before my eyes. I noticed the characters were shapes I recognised and I understood them to be Hebrew letters. They were moving with the pages but also seemed to be moving and vibrant with life themselves. The Lord began to speak in this room and said that He had brought me here to understand the codex of nations. Codex was not a word I knew. I discovered the meaning later following this encounter: it is an ancient manuscript in book form. I was seeing it, one page after the other, moving before me. After a time the individual letters began to move off the pages and increase in size. They became huge—probably triple my height, imposing. They were three dimensional, animated with sound coming from them all. I was drawn to one particular character and the Lord then said to me, 'Sit on My Word.' This was incredible because, in the spirit, I could actually climb this letter and sit on it. I lay back, feeling its astonishing sound and resonance vibrating life beneath me.

I discovered later that I was sitting on the Hebrew character *pey* which means 'breath, speech and word'. As I lay back into this letter, I was literally subsumed by it. Falling into it as it became marshmallow- then liquid-like. I came through the letter into a spacious place in the spirit realm. There the Lord began to speak to me about the 'Word made flesh' in us as His people who are in Christ Jesus. The understanding of this truth went deep within me.

I was then catapulted into a deeper realm of the spirit where the reality of this truth—which I knew through reading the Bible—was then literally marked and burned into me. My back was burning with incredible heat in the spirit; yet at the same time, I felt the intense, searing heat where I was in the earthly seen realm. Here the Lord spoke to me further about being burned and marked with His Word. We read about God marking His people with His Word in Ezekiel 8, where a scribe of the Lord is commanded to mark those who had been lamenting at the sin of Israel. This mark was placed on the forehead with the *tav* Hebrew character so they would not be killed in God's judgment. The *tav* was the shape of a cross in this era of the Hebrew language. Is that not incredible?

In this case, God marked me with the letter *pey*, the character of His Word and breath. Following this burning process, the Lord brought me back to the room with the table on which the codex had been transformed into a vibrant green, grass-like material which was fully alive. I was told to wrap this word around me and wear it. As I did this, it became a covering for my entire body in the spirit.

Strange though this personal encounter was, and possibly is for you on reading it, the unseen reality of the spirit is open for those who hunger for greater understanding and knowledge of God and His Word. These deep spiritual experiences reveal greater understanding of the Word of God and allow us to live more fully alive in them.

This encounter transformed and expounded my understanding of Scripture to a whole new level and fastened me into truth like never before. I could feel the weight of God's Word in me and upon me from that point on. Such a profound encounter opened my spirit and senses to reading the Word of God with a fresh perspective that I would not have had otherwise. The ways of God are not ours, but He invites us into them. The Lord has encounters for you in the spirit realm that will give greater understanding and knowledge to His truth for you. The truth of God will be revealed and sustained in you and through you via intense experiences like this one in the spirit with the Lord. We must run to God's truth and desire it.

Truth Is Available

Buy truth and do not sell it—wisdom, instruction and understanding as well (Proverbs 23:23).

The door to truth is open through Christ Jesus. It is narrow yet expansive and is without end. The breadth of the spirit realm is open to us, just as the unchartered territory was to the explorers of old. As Kingdom pioneers, we are called to push beyond the perceived known limits into the unknown.

I am intrigued by the great explorer Ernest Shackleton (1874–1922). His drive and focus led him to be part of, as well as leading, numerous expeditions to the South Pole. He had such determination in him, returning year after year undeterred to go even further into uncharted territory. We too must have the same grit and determination to keep pursuing the Lord and His ways and never to give in.

Shackleton's main aim was to explore the Antarctic from the Weddell Sea to McMurdo Sound via the South Pole. On the way his ship, well named *Endurance,* became trapped, drifting with the ice flow for ten months before being completely crushed as the ice moved. Incredibly, members of the expedition drifted on ice floes for another five months with limited supplies and materials for warmth. They finally escaped in boats to Elephant Island in the South Shetland Islands, where they subsisted on seal meat and penguins.

With amazing fortitude, Shackleton and five others navigated a 16-day journey over 800 miles (1,300 km) to South Georgia in a whaling boat (basically a 6.9 metre double-ended rowing boat). Four months later, after leading four separate relief expeditions, Shackleton succeeded in rescuing his crew from Elephant Island. Almost two years later not one of Shackleton's crew from the *Endurance* had died. Is this determination not inspiring?

Shackleton and his men came close to the end numerous times. Following his epic adventure he wrote: 'We had seen God in his splendours, heard the test that nature render. We had reached the naked soul of man.'[1]

This pushing beyond one's known limits causes a supernatural, miraculous extension into the unknown. We need to absorb the unknown, learning from people like Shackleton—people who know, when faced with challenges, that determination, endurance and perseverance are required. Let us be like him and respond to his exhortation to: '...put the footprint of courage into the stirrup of patience.'[2]

Let us be fearless and bold in Christ, to move *to* the Lord and *with* the Lord into the realms set apart for us to experience and encounter, giving us greater understanding of the truth of God. This exploration mandate never ends due to the nature of our God who is fathomless and never-ending. Today, the Lord invites you through and beyond the open door into greater understanding.

ACTIVATION: ENTER INTO THE REALM OF KNOWLEDGE

There are multiple rooms filled with revelation and understanding that are open to you. These rooms are like libraries, filled with books, papers and scrolls to be read and received. Each one is unique to you: designed for you and the understanding the Lord desires to be yours. Comprehension will come to you as you sit in these places of learning. The door is open.

RESPONSE AND ACTIVATION

Find a quiet space and time to sit with the Lord. Allow your response to Jesus to be a desire for learning and comprehension by His Spirit to yours. As Jesus comes close, speak to Him about what is in your heart and hear His answer to you. Do not rush. Take time to sit with Him and then ask Him to show you the rooms that have been set apart for your learning, discernment and perception. As you ask Jesus these questions, expect to be shown these places available to you. Unique to you. You will find yourself in a room.

- Take note of what it feels like and looks like. What is its atmosphere?
- Who is in the room with you? What is their role, and do you need to ask them for help?
- Ask the Lord what He desires for you to receive from this place today. Take time to watch, listen and take in all the Lord is opening to you.
- In what form is the revelation and knowledge coming to you being given? Take time to receive and absorb all that the Lord has given to you. Write it down if necessary and keep your attention and spiritual senses focused on the room.
- Ask the Lord if there is any more understanding that He desires to bring you into today. Anything more for you to see or hear. Take time to watch and listen with the Lord there.
- Is there something else the Lord would like to give you or tell you here?

Ask Him how often you can come back to this place of learning and if there is more He wants to show you today. This 'knowledge realm' is one of many open to us as we look and see beyond what we know and what is in the natural, earth realm. Be curious and courageous: ask the Lord continually to show you more and be bold enough to step through the door that is open in the spirit to you. That door remains open to you as you pursue more of God with a pure heart.

Continue to go beyond, feel and see beyond all your previous experiences. Determine to train your senses in the unseen realm regularly. You were made for adventure and to be a pioneer. There is much to explore and experience. This is just the beginning.

My Prayer for You

Lord Jesus, I pray for this dear reader—that You would take this person into the places You have prepared at this time, places of deep closeness and affection with You. That You would lead this reader on a journey and adventure of ever-increasing vibrancy and joy of life in You.

Dear friend, I bless you to enter into the depths of relationship with Jesus and to move in the depths of the Spirit, to know Him more in increasing measure, day by day. I bless you to experience the power, light and life of Christ Jesus in the unseen realm and to see beyond all previous limitations. To know you are one with Him and to move and abide with Him in all realms. I bless you into a life of supernatural encounter that takes you to a place of dwelling with the Lord in a new way. I pray that you and your life will reveal the glorious luminescent light of God's glory and transform others' lives as you do this.

See beyond, my friend. Go beyond in Christ and flourish.

ENDNOTES

1. Ernest Shackleton, *South: The ENDURANCE Expedition* (New York: Signet Books, 1999).
2. Ibid.

ADDITIONAL RESOURCES

The Divinity Code: The Keys to Decoding Your Dreams and Visions by Adrian Beale and Adam F. Thompson

Angel Armies by Tim Sheets

The Prophetic Warrior by Emma Stark

ABOUT THE AUTHOR

Sarah-Jane Biggart is Lead Seer Prophet at Global Prophetic Alliance (GPA) and Director of the GPA Prayer Institute. She is ordained with Christian International. Her passion is equipping, training and demonstrating the fullness of who God is, the spiritual gifts available to all believers, the reality of access to the realm of the Spirit and how to navigate it for Kingdom advancement on earth in all spheres of life and work.

Sarah-Jane lives in Central Scotland, UK, with her husband Alastair and children and works from Glasgow, Scotland, with the Global Prophetic Alliance. She spends much of her time undertaking the hidden work of the Kingdom, prophesying and releasing spiritual strategy to leaders and reformers in various spheres of society internationally. In addition to raising cohorts and armies of spiritual warfare and strategic prayer, she focuses her time on praying in and for nations behind the scenes.

You can follow Sarah-Jane at Global Prophetic Alliance, home of Glasgow Prophetic Centre, on YouTube, Facebook and Instagram. Sarah-Jane also hosts 'World Prayer Watch' on the GPA channels.

Personal Public Facebook Page:
@sarahjanebiggart10
Instagram:
sarahjanebiggart_

For further information about Sarah-Jane and specific details regarding speaking invitations please go to www.propheticscots.com.